HEARING GOD'S VOICE INTELLIGENTLY

DR. RUDI SWANEPOEL

𝒢

God's Glory
Media
Atlanta, GA

Hearing God's Voice Intelligently
ISBN: 978-0-9772647-1-1
Copyright © 2008 by Rudi Swanepoel
P. O. Box 1430, Dacula, GA 30019
www.GodsGlory.org

TABLE OF CONTENTS

ACKNOWLEDGEMENTS

To Almighty God - the loving, revealing, communicating and personal God that You are. For stirring my heart, teaching my spirit and directing my actions to write this book for Your glory.

And as always to my loving wife Sharon – For exploring with me the many dimensions and multi facetted realms of divine revelation, eagerly pursuing God's every promise for us with that unwavering confidence that the Holy Spirit alone can give.

To our fellow Kingdom Builders – For your passion to further the Kingdom of God, your faithful support to God's Glory Ministries and for partnering with us to content for lost souls around the world.

ENDORSEMENTS

The Lord promised to bring a great revival in these last days and there is so much confusion and uncertainty in the world. We must hear the voice of God clearly and be lead by the Lord. I am convinced that every step we take is very important and we should be careful not to miss the leading and the direction of the Lord.

I have known Rudi & Sharon Swanepoel and I know they fear the Lord and hear His voice. And I am sure you will be greatly helped as you read this book. May God make His voice so clear to all of us; through the Holy Spirit because there are many strange voices in the world and sadly in the church.

Dr. Bahjat & Nina Batarseh, D.min, Th.D, Ph.D, D.Lett, D.D, D.Ed, D.Coun, C.R.P.S.
The Way of Light Ministries
Dr. Bahjat Batarseh Ministries Inc.
International Evangelists

Timely, Practical, Biblical are all descriptions of this outstanding book. At a time when there are so many voices, how can I hear and know God's voice? This book will help you hear and understand the only voice that counts; God's!

Rudi has given us a field manual to hearing the only voice that matters. I heartily recommend this book.
Ron Johnson, Senior Pastor
Bethel Temple Church
Hampton, VA

I heard Rudi preach the first time in the Republic of Georgia. I was leading a Vision trip of leading American pastors to this former communist country, to help them build a Bible School. Revival was in the air and trained pastors were desperately needed, to carry on the work of the Holy Spirit. During the pastors' conference that we had been invited to preach, Rudi rose to speak. From the moment he began, the crowd was in awe. They had never heard preaching like that. Quite frankly, although I was raised in a preachers' home, and I had listened to some of the greats, I had never heard anything like it either. Wow. What insights Rudi had.

And now, several years later, he keeps getting better and better. In an age when local church evangelism is almost non-existent, Rudi's schedule is jam-packed. Rudi is special, his message is special, and his latest book "Hearing God's Voice Intelligently" is very special. Be blessed, as you hear anew God speaking to you.

Sam Johnson
Executive Director
Priority One

FOREWORD

I have not spoken in secret, in a corner of the land of darkness; I did not call the descendants of Jacob [to a fruitless service], saying, Seek Me for nothing [but I promised them a just reward]. I, the Lord, speak righteousness (the truth — trustworthy, straightforward correspondence between deeds and words); I declare things that are right[1].

To you it has been given to know the secrets and mysteries of the kingdom of heaven, but to them it has not been given. For whoever has [spiritual knowledge], to him will more be given and he will be furnished richly so that he will have abundance; but from him who has not, even what he has will be taken away. This is the reason that I speak to them in parables: because having the power of seeing, they do not see; and having the power of hearing, they do not hear, nor do they grasp and understand[2].

---

[1] Isaiah 45:19 AMP
[2] Matthew 13:11-13 AMP

And I know that His commandment is (means) eternal life. So whatever I speak, I am saying [exactly] what My Father has told Me to say and in accordance with His instructions.[3]

For I know the thoughts and plans that I have for you, says the Lord, thoughts and plans for welfare and peace and not for evil, to give you hope in your final outcome.[4]

Call to Me and I will answer you and show you great and mighty things, fenced in and hidden, which you do not know (do not distinguish and recognize, have knowledge of and understand).[5]

- God

---

[3] John 12:50 AMP
[4] Jeremiah 29:11 AMP
[5] Jeremiah 33:3 AMP.

PREFACE

Heaven is not a silent place. Its throne room is filled with noise. The character of God is to commune, to share, and to express. To talk to the ones He loves. Throughout the pages of the Bible we find God in conversation with people. We call the sacred book the word of God. It is God's communication with humanity!

When God speaks everyone that hears His voice listens. His voice carries creative power. His very words cause a fusion of atoms, a creation of substance, an appearing of that which has never been onto the scene of the present. He said:

"Let there be light and there was light."[6]

Simple, yet effective. The Bible does not say where the light came from. Remember the sun was not yet created. The voice of God is not

---

[6] Genesis 1:3

only heard but felt and seen. It knows no boundaries, is limitless in power and does the impossible. The moment they are formed, His words set out to accomplish precisely what the heart of God intended.

> *"Out of the abundance of the heart, the mouth speaks."*[7]

His words never fall to the ground becoming useless; giving up on the task at hand. They're not idle. They know no neutrality. They flow in the direction He spoke them with one purpose in mind: "We must accomplish what we were created to do."

Ability to speak and to listen
The ability to speak presupposes the ability to listen. How can you talk if you cannot hear? Effective communication warrants transmitters and receivers, ears and a mouth, projector and screen, pen and paper. Almighty God can do both! He speaks and listens. In fact, nothing escapes His ears! He is aware of every word, whisper and thought ever made!

> *God's voice knows no boundaries; is limitless in power and does the impossible.*

---

[7] Matthew 12:34

10

Amazingly He also made you with the ability to communicate. Not only with others on this level of our natural existence, but also with Him on the level of His spiritual existence.

"God is a Spirit and where the Spirit of the Lord is there is liberty."[8]

The Lord has given you freedom to; among other things express yourself freely. You have received the ability to speak words He listens to and hear words He speaks! This is remarkable. People come standard with this built-in ability. You do not need an upgrade to hear God's voice. You do not need a separate attachment or some other thing. You are equipped to communicate with the Creator of heaven and earth!

Communication is not always verbal. Pictures talk. A great artist has the ability to do with a picture what a poet can do with a paragraph. The Lord does not always use words when He speaks. Sometimes He speaks in pictures, dreams, visions, thoughts, actions and impressions. He employs a variety of media, audio-visual and evocative methods to get His messages across. In this book we will explore many of them. We will learn how to listen for

---

[8] 2 Corinthians 3:17

and hear the voice of God. We will learn to develop a sensitive ear along with a sharp spirit and clear mind to commune with Almighty God in a regular and profound way.

We will explore the five spiritual senses you received from the Lord while we position our lives for encounters with the Lord, encounters that will transform our lives, make deposits into our souls and bring divine order to our existence. Your ability to hear the voice of the Lord and obey it is directly connected to the blessings God wants to bestow on your life.

> *"If you will diligently listen to the voice of the Lord your God, being watchful to do all His commandments which I command you this day. . . all these blessings shall come upon you and overtake you if you heed the voice of the Lord your God."[9]*

Together we will discover the awesome power even one word from God can have; a declaration from Heaven powerful enough that it will cause a flow of purposeful direction, focused vision and defined destiny in our lives.

---

[9] Deuteronomy 28:1-2 AMP

CHAPTER 1
THE CHARACTER OF THE VOICE OF GOD

*T*he **voice** of the Lord is upon the waters; the God of glory thunders; the Lord is upon many (great) waters. The **voice** of the Lord is powerful; the **voice** of the Lord is full of majesty. The **voice** of the Lord breaks the cedars; yes, the Lord breaks in pieces the cedars of Lebanon. He makes them also to skip like a calf; Lebanon and Sirion (Mount Hermon) like a young, wild ox. The **voice** of the Lord splits and flashes forth forked lightning. The **voice** of the Lord makes the wilderness tremble; the Lord shakes the Wilderness of Kadesh. The **voice** of the Lord makes the hinds bring forth their young, and His **voice** strips bare the forests,

> *while in His temple everyone is saying, Glory!*[10]

King David was looking across the landscape of the Holy Land and saw a thunder storm approaching. Dark clouds were billowing in the wind and the brilliant flashes of lightning illuminated the surrounding area. It could have been just another storm, but as David peered into the storm he saw a marvelous revelation of the character of the voice of the Lord.

His voice upon the waters
Let's look firstly at the word "voice" in this passage. The Hebrew word here is *"qowl"*. It means "to call aloud; a voice or a sound; thundering"[11] This word is descriptive of much more than mere words. In fact, sound travels at a speed of 1,142 feet per second. This is known as the speed of sound. For the purpose of this study I want you to know that there is a speed connected to the voice of the Lord. When He speaks, His words travel towards you swiftly and powerfully! Light also travels at a specific speed. Light beats sound every time! It travels much faster. It takes a few seconds for the boom of a lightning strike to reach your ear after its sight reached your eye.

---

[10] Psalm 29:3-9 AMP Emphasis added
[11] Strong's Exhaustive Concordance of the Bible, OT 6963

Now let's look at David's first statement of the voice of the Lord in Psalm 29:3:

The voice of the Lord is upon the waters.

The waters he was referring to was not the "lower" waters, i.e. the oceans, rivers or lakes. According to the Hebrew word used here he was referring to the "higher" waters. The voice of the Lord is upon the clouds; the moisture in the air. Remember he received this revelation while looking at a thunder storm. Think for a minute what he is saying to us.

About 2000 years ago there was a flash of Light; a holy lightning bolt that struck in the spirit realm on a hill called Calvary just outside of Jerusalem. Jesus, the Light of the world reached deep into the depravity of humanity by paying the full price of sin. The energy and power released on that cross was enough to rescue every person who would ever walk the face of the earth.

> . . .and we [actually] saw His
> glory (His honor, His majesty),
> such glory as an only begotten
> son receives from his father, full

> *of grace (favor, loving-kindness)*
> *and truth.*[12]

Ever since that wondrous day we have been hearing the rumblings and thundering of the revelation of that blessed event. We saw the Light and now He is being revealed in an ongoing sound emanating from heaven.

> *God, who at various times and in*
> *various ways spoke in time past to*
> *the fathers by the prophets, has in*
> *these last days spoken to us by*
> *His Son, whom He has appointed*
> *heir of all things, through whom*
> *also He made the worlds; who*
> *being the brightness of His glory*
> *and the express image of His*
> *person, and upholding all things*
> *by the word of His power, when*
> *He had by Himself purged our*
> *sins, sat down at the right hand of*
> *the Majesty on high,*[13]

Everything He reveals today is in some way connected to what Jesus did on the cross for you and me. This revelation is progressive and becomes more glorious as it "rolls" towards us

---

[12] John 1:14b AMP
[13] Hebrews 1:1-3 NKJV

in ever increasing volume and intensity, just like thunder that rides on the clouds in the rain.

His Voice is Powerful

The Hebrew word used here is "koach". Literally the word means "firm / vigor". Figuratively it means "capacity / means / produce"[14]. The sounds of revelation coming from the Lord are powerful! They are firm and vigorous! They have a quality in them that produce. The fruit attached to them are *His voice accomplishes everything and anything!* abundant, ripe, sweet and satisfying. His voice carries creative power! They are not empty. They have a tremendous capacity! They are so much more than mere words. They carry, among other things, visions, dreams, pictures, illuminations, impressions, revelations, emotions, promise, hope and love. They are not poor. They possess means! Resources that will meet your greatest need! They have wealth that causes the poor to be rich. His voice accomplishes everything and anything!

Next time God speaks to you bear in mind what is happening. His words bring into your spirit a new capacity to receive all that Heaven has.

---

[14] Strong's Exhaustive Dictionary of Bible Words: OT: 3581

17

They bring forth a wealth that cannot be counted in currency. They cause your spiritual life to become fruitful to produce exactly what the Lord intended and willed over your life!

His Voice is Full of Majesty

Majesty here means "magnificence / excellence"[15]. This word comes from the root word that means "to swell up"[16]. The voice of the Lord deals with big things. When the Lord speaks over you the small stuff seems to fade into obscurity. His voice will enhance the great priorities of the Spirit over your life. John exclaims:

He must increase but I must decrease.
[He must grow more prominent; I must grow
less so][17]

There are things in your life that needs to fade away. Things you might think are important to your spiritual existence might not even fit into the bigger picture of God over your life. Our plans must play second fiddle to the awesome plans of God for our lives. Our emotions must be subject to the heartbeat of God. Our thoughts are not His thoughts. They must simply make way for the infinite wisdom and revelation of

---

[15] Strong's Exhaustive Dictionary of Bible Words: OT: 1926
[16] Strong's Exhaustive Dictionary of Bible Words: OT: 1921
[17] John 3:30 AMP

the words of God. The list goes on and on. When you listen to the voice of the Lord its majesty will cause the proper "swelling up" of all the Lord delights in. Attributes, tendencies and destinies will grow as a result of the word of the Lord spoken over your life.

His Voice Breaks the Cedars

The cedars of ancient Lebanon are legendary. Many a writer, inspired by the Holy Spirit, has used the cedars in metaphors throughout the Old Testament. In fact they are mentioned 75 times in the Bible. In the context of our text a better choice could hardly be found. To fully understand what is being revealed to us and how it is connected to the voice of the Lord, we have to examine the cedar.

They are formidable. They grow to a height of up to 120 feet. They are thirsty. They drink about 30 gallons of water every day. They are "selfish". Nothing grows or shares the ground under them. They are tenacious. Their roots are very strong and well developed. They grow in ancient Lebanon. The word Lebanon comes from the root word that means: "heart"[18].

Walk with me through the revelation and application as it applies to our subject matter.

---

[18] Strong's Exhaustive Dictionary of Bible Words: OT: 3823

There are things growing in our hearts, our Lebanons that are every bit as formidable as those giant cedars David referred to. These things can be unholy emotions like anger, bitterness and rage. They can grow in our hearts to represent past experiences, defeats and failures, even disappointments. They can even represent sin; everything opposing God's plans and purposes for our lives. These "trees" can occupy large portions of our daily existence, keeping our attention away from the many wondrous opportunities the Lord brings our way. These things can be very thirsty. They drink up all the moisture and life-sap we need to maintain a vigorous, successful and satisfying life. When they take root in our Lebanon (heart) they

When He speaks over your life every stronghold, every thought, every emotion that opposes His plans and purposes is obliterated.

drive out any other forms of life from our hearts, wanting to dominate our mind and emotions. Their roots are often well developed and they are oh so difficult to remove. Many seek professional assistance and counseling, hoping to find the right tools to clear the affected areas of their hearts. They hope to find chainsaws, ropes and stump-grinders to get the job done. It is an arduous and long process.

Friend there is a better way! The voice of the Lord can break the cedars growing in your heart! When He speaks over your life every stronghold, every thought, every emotion that opposes His plans and purposes is obliterated. His voice creates a clearing in your heart for the seed of His word to be planted and to flourish in you. Isn't this amazing? Will you tune you ears to hear that powerful voice coming from the throne room of heaven? But wait there is even more.

> *He makes them also to skip like a calf; Lebanon and Sirion (Mount Hermon) like a young, wild ox.*[19]

At the sound of the voice of the Lord what is rigid becomes flexible. What is seemingly dead comes alive. Things inactive are activated, those normally unmoving becomes pliable. This is a wonderful thought. It makes me think of a farm in South Africa I visited many times as a boy. During one visit, the farmer started the process of weaning the calves from their mothers. They had to learn to no longer depend on the milk of the cow, but to find their sustenance in the field and the water trough. The farmer herded all the calves into a small enclosure. They no longer had free access to their food supply hanging

---

[19] Psalm 29:6 AMP.

under their mother's bellies. All they had in that small enclosure was straw and water. At first they moaned into the night hours. They were restless. Their once care-free life drifted beyond the reaches of their short term memory. With every passing day they became more docile and quiet. It seemed as if life was being drained from them. Have you ever felt like this? Can you identify with these "poor" calves? Their longing for mother's milk slowly made way for an even deeper need, freedom. They missed their milk, but they missed the open pastures even more. The open fields were now beckoning beyond the wired fence. At last, the farmer opened the gate of the small enclosure. They were free to once again frolic among the cows in the field. I wish you were there with me as I watched those calves. They skipped and danced around for what seemed like hours. They played and darted around in a calved-craze. Amazingly not one of them returned to the cows for milk. They ate the sweet grass of the field and drank of the fresh cold water that was pumped into the trough.

The voice of the Lord releases you from the small enclosures and boundaries that abound in your life. It releases a freedom over you to rejoice and dance in jubilation over the glory of your God. He indeed leads us beside still waters and takes us to green pastures!

His Voice Flashes forth Forked Lightning
The lightshow nature can put on with lightning and thunder supersedes any fireworks display man can come up with. It is truly spectacular, especially on a dark night in an open field. I have seen lightning appear on the eastern horizon and run across the expanse of the night sky. Forking tongues of illuminated energy to the north and south were able to cause the night to momentarily disappear in a brightness that rivals the noon sun. Then it continued to shoot towards the western horizon at lightning speed and vanished behind a thunder cloud. The sound generated by this bolt was riding on its coattails, unable to keep up. Light made way to sound. I was left with an awe-inspiring sense of the power inside one lightning strike.

In fact, I am in good company. Charles Spurgeon, also known as the prince of preachers, marveled at the weather also:

> *When God is abroad I love to walk out in some wide space and to look up and mark the opening gates of heaven, as the lightning reveals far beyond and enables me to gaze into the unseen. I like*

> *to hear my Father's voice vibrate in the thunder.*[20]

How does this enhance our study of the voice of God? Well David said:

> *The **voice** of the Lord splits and flashes forth forked lightning. The **voice** of the Lord makes the wilderness tremble; the Lord shakes the Wilderness of Kadesh.*[21]

His Light

The voice of the Lord always produces light. In Genesis the Lord said:

> *Let there be light. And there was light.*[22]

When the Lord speaks into your life, His words will illuminate your being. When He answers your questions, His answers will shine as the morning sun. Every shadow disappears over every area He addresses. There are no shadows cast in His turning.[23] In fact He dwells in

---

[20] Hero's of the Faith: Charles Spurgeon, p 48
[21] Psalm 29:7-8 AMP.
[22] Genesis 1:3
[23] James 1:17

unapproachable light.[24] He is the Light and there is no darkness in Him.[25]

The voice of the Lord places things in complete perspective. It illuminates and reveals that which is formerly unseen. When released into the expanse of your heart, every area basks in the brightness of the word. The voice of the Lord is seen before it is heard because light travels much faster than sound. Generated from the heart of God in the Throne Room of heaven, His voice travels great distances to reach you. It pierces the darkness, traverses the pages of the Bible, penetrates your natural existence and separates your soul-realm from your spirit, a great feat indeed.

> *For the Word that God speaks is alive and full of power [making it active, operative, energizing, and effective]; it is sharper than any two-edged sword, **penetrating to the dividing line of the breath of life (soul) and [the immortal] spirit**, and of joints and marrow [of the deepest parts of our nature], exposing and sifting and analyzing and judging the very*

---

[24] 1 Timothy 6:16
[25] 1 John 1:5-7

thoughts and purposes of the heart. [26]

His voice clarifies the purposes of your heart and thoughts. His voice exposes your motives and desires. It eliminates all confusion and makes things crisp and clear. Before you listen to the voice of the Lord, open your eyes to see His voice. You'll see His light before you hear His sound.

*My son, attend to my words; consent and submit to my sayings. Let them not depart from your **sight**; keep them in the center of your heart.* [27]

Again, the words that God speaks are here connected to our sight and not just to our hearing ability. *Let them not depart from your sight.*

His Sound
The sound of His voice is awesome. It is load even when whispered. It is clear even in the presence of background

His voice clarifies the purposes of your heart and thoughts

[26] Hebrews 4:12 Emphasis Added
[27] Proverbs 4:20–21 AMP. Emphasis Added

noise. The sound of His voice is your second exposure to what He says. First you saw the light of His words penetrate your darkness, now you hear the sound of His voice resonating through the depths of your spirit. When you saw the light you expected the sound and it came!

The sound of God's voice is reassuring like that of a Father, instructive like that of a Teacher, directing like that of a Guide, authoritative like that of King, compassionate like that of a Physician and loving like that of a Lover. His voice is also a singing voice. Did you know that the Lord even sings over you?

> *. . . . He will exult over you with singing.*[28]

The sound of His voice is distinctively recognizable. One of the ways we recognize a person is by knowing the sound of their voice. After many years of blissful marriage to my lovely wife, Sharon, I can recognize her voice in an instant, whether on the phone, or listening to a CD, on the TV or in another room. She cannot mask her voice enough to hide her identity from me. I know her too well. You are likewise able to familiarize yourself with the sound of His voice by getting to know your God

---

[28] Zephaniah 3:17b AMP

in a deep, personal and intimate way. Your knowledge of the sound of His voice becomes invaluable to you. No matter how He chooses to manifest His words to you, you'll know them by their sound in your spirit! You'll quickly identify imposters and impersonators. No one can sound like the Lord. Do you know Him like that? Is your relationship with Jesus so strong, so intimate that you know the sound of His voice? If not, what are you waiting for? Perk up your ears and listen. Open up your heart to the sound of His voice.

His Power

> *The voice of the Lord makes the wilderness tremble; the Lord shakes the wilderness of Kadesh.*[29]

The Hebrew word for tremble here means "to dance / to twist / to whirl / to travail"[30]. As David watched the amazing power of a thunderstorm rolling over the wilderness he describes the power as causing the wilderness to tremble. Trees shook as nature responded to the raw power of thunder and lightning. They swayed in the wind like dancers on the rhythm

---

[29] Psalm 29:8
[30] Strong's Exhaustive Dictionary of Bible Words: OT: 2342

of music. It is an interesting choice of words here because it also means to travail. Can it be that the voice of the Lord causes new life to spring forth? My answer is a resounding YES!

The voice of the Lord unlocks new life. It activates a birthing process over the regions it is released. Interestingly the Hebrew word for wilderness here is *midbar*. According to the Strong's dictionary *midbar* by implication means a desert and also speech![31] When the voice of the Lord is spoken into your life it also affects your *midbar*. The arid desert areas of your life as well as your speech! It causes your words to bring forth new life. The impact of the voice of the Lord upon our speech cannot be over stated. Reinhard Bonnke, the German evangelist whom the Lord has used to bring the Gospel to multiple millions says: *God's word in your mouth is just as powerful as God's word in His mouth.* When you speak the words that God speaks power is released. It could be in quoting a scripture or repeating a prophetic promise or even reminding the Lord of a specific promise. He says in His word:

> . . . *you who [are His servants and by your prayers] put the Lord*

---

[31] Strong's Exhaustive Dictionary of Bible Words: OT: 4057

in remembrance [of His promises], keep not silence, [32]

There is something special about the audible utterance of God's promises over your life. Apply this verse by putting the Lord in remembrance of His promises. Do not be silent! Actually God does not suffer from memory loss. He knows what He said and will do what He said. When you repeat what He said over your life, your audible words release a power of agreement and alignment over your faculties. They will submit and align with your faith in accordance to the words the Lord has spoken over your life.

Not only is there power released in the voice of the Lord that is connected to your speech, but Psalm 29:8 adds another descriptive

> **Our words carry the holiness of the Lord.**

word over the region that trembles and shakes at the voice of the Lord. He says: *the Lord shakes the Wilderness of Kadesh.*

The Hebrew word *Kadesh* means *holy* or *consecrated*[33]. According to the Strong's

---

[32] Isaiah 62:6b AMP

[33] McClintock & Strong Encyclopedia; Reference –Ka'desh

Dictionary it also means *sanctuary*. This is very exciting to me. We have already established that there is a tremendous power in the voice of the Lord connected to our speech. Now the definition becomes even more specific. The Lord shakes a specific wilderness; a specific type of "speech" if you will. Remember the Hebrew word *wilderness* by implication means speech. This wilderness's name is Kadesh; a holy, consecrated place, even a place of sanctuary. This wilderness was the place where the Israelites camped on their way to the Promised Land. Before the name of this place meant *Fountain of Judgment*[34]. When the tabernacle of the Lord stood on the place it became Kadesh, holy and consecrated place! So many times our speech can be a fountain of judgment. Our words render judgment in so many areas. We voice our opinions weather asked or not. We speak things over other's lives and efforts without ever thinking twice at the consequences. When the Lord's voice is heard over our "Fountain of Judgment" it becomes our "Kadesh". Our speech becomes holy speech. Our words carry the holiness of the Lord.

The time has come for our speech to be shaken by the voice of the Lord! May we utter words of

---

[34] Ibid

holiness, consecrated in the presence of the Lord.

The voice of the Lord makes the hinds bring forth their young

We have already touched on this new life aspect of the voice of the Lord when we looked at His power. Now I want us to look at it a little closer.

> *The voice of the Lord makes the hinds bring forth their young*[35]

When God speaks creation happens. New life springs forth. Birthing takes place. In this verse the Psalmist uses the same Hebrew word as in the previous verse. In verse 8 it was translated *tremble* and *shake*. Now it speaks of new birth! At the sound of His voice the hinds give birth. We can look at the hinds here as symbolic of the people of God. The Lord says that He will make *your feet like hinds' feet for the high places*[36]. The Psalmist also compares his hunger for more of God to the thirsting of the deer.[37]

When the Lord speaks over our lives it brings forth new life to our spirits. His voice causes the birthing of new dreams, vision, destinies, hope, love, peace, power, etc. in our lives. Do you

---

[35] Psalm 29:9a AMP

[36] 2 Samuel 22:34 , Psalm 18:33, Habakkuk 3:19

[37] Psalm 42:1

need new life in your spirit? Would you like to have new directions, purpose and a sense of destiny? Allow the Lord to speak over your life! Welcome the sound of His voice into your life. One word from the Lord will turn barrenness into fertility. It will generate new life in a depleted heart. Cause new hope to spring up amidst an atmosphere of defeat and failure. The voice of the Lord is directly connected to your spiritual legacy. It will cause you to bring forth your spiritual sons and daughters; your own Timothys and Esthers. The voice of the Lord in your life will secure the future of the next generation. Your influence will be perpetuated past the days of your life here on earth!

The voice of the Lord strips bare the forests.
Here we find another amazing action of the voice of the Lord. It *strips bare the forests*[38] The Hebrew word for *strips* is *chasaph* and means to *strip off / to make naked / to clean / to discover*[39]

The voice of the Lord has a way to rip off all of our pretenses. It unmasks us. It strips us bare to where the naked truth lies within us. It reveals the real us. Many people do not like this quality of the voice of the Lord. They have

---

[38] Psalm 29:9b AMP
[39] Stong's Dictionary Hebrew #2834

33

painstakingly covered their true self with many protective layers of image and desire as to conceal the very weaknesses and inabilities God endeavors to reveal. God will always reveal to heal! He never exposes to hurt, ridicule or refuse. His voice in your life will cut through the chase. It will peal off the layers of life until the real you are bare in the warm atmosphere of His love and presence.

There are so many "plants" that have taken over in our lives. Deadly emotions grow as overgrowth of spiritual forests, shrinking the fruitful fields of our hearts; anger, bitterness, rage, un-forgiveness, etc. Then there are other things like temptations and distractions that spring up like weeds to

God's voice forges into the uncharted territories of our hearts and souls and causes us to discover God's true plans and purposes for our lives.

choke the life out of us. What about weaknesses, sicknesses, brokenness and more. The list goes on an on. God's voice has a clearing effect on our lives. It strips these malicious forests bare. It exposes them and helps us to get detangled from their reach.

Chasaph also means *to discover*. I love this one! The voice of the Lord also causes discovery to take place in our lives! It forges into the uncharted territories of our hearts and souls and causes us to discover God's true plans and purposes for our lives. Are you ready to uncover things in you, you never knew existed? Allow the Lord to speak over your life. Follow the echoes of His voice to these regions of your soul. Let His voice lead you to know more about yourself.

Chasaph can lastly be translated *to clean*. The voice of the Lord has a cleansing power that is truly remarkable. It cleans our hearts and motives even our thoughts and intentions.

> *So that He might sanctify her, having cleansed her by the washing of water with the Word,*[40]

Here the Word of the Lord is referred to as water. The bride of Christ, the Church, is cleansed by the washing of the Word. How else will we be presented to Him undefiled and clean? Not only are we cleansed by the blood of the Lamb, but also by the Word of the Lord!

---

[40] Ephesians 5:26 AMP

In this first chapter we have already learned so much about the character of the voice of the Lord, and we are just getting started. The Psalmist ends his discourse on the voice of the Lord in Psalm 29: 9b with a very powerful statement.

> . . . *while in His temple everyone*
> *is saying, Glory!*[41]

The voice of the Lord brings His Glory to your whole being. The apostle Paul clearly states in the New Testament that our bodies are a *temple of God* and that *the Holy Spirit dwells in us.* [42] When we hear the voice of the Lord in our lives, it ushers in His Glory in a phenomenal way. Every fiber of your being will declare the Glory of God in response to hearing His voice. Every part of you will be involved. Your emotions, your thoughts, your actions, your heart's motives, everything! In His temple (your body) everyone will say: Glory! When the Lord reveals His voice to you, and you yield to all He says and declares over your life, it will bring tremendous glory to His name. His voice brings intense praise, awe and adoration into your life.

---

[41] Psalm 29:9 b AMP
[42] 1 Corinthians 3:16

Everything should eventually point to the Glory of God. In the end, it's all for His Glory. When we identify, yield to and obey the voice of the Lord, we position ourselves to declare, carry and display the Glory of the Lord. Then and only then can we fulfill the ultimate purpose for our being. We were created for His glory!

> *Even everyone who is called by My name, **whom I have created for My glory**, whom I have formed, whom I have made.* [43]

---

[43] Isaiah 43:7 AMP. Emphasis Added

Hearing God's Voice Intelligently

CHAPTER 2
VARIETY OF THE VOICE OF THE LORD

The voice of the Lord comes to us in a variety of ways. God is not limited to communicate to us just verbally or audibly. In fact experts recognize that people too communicate in many ways. We write, we talk, we do and we draw. We create and project. We spend a great deal of our time finding new and effective ways to get our messages across.

Why then do we want to limit God to only communicate His messages to us in a certain way? Why do we limit ourselves by only accepting and receiving His wisdom and power in ways that we are familiar and comfortable with? In this chapter we will look at various valid ways the Lord uses to communicate to us.

Words

Let's deal with the obvious first. The voice of the Lord comes to us in the form of words. We are people of The Book. The Bible is the inspired word of God. He revealed in it His will, plans and actions for humanity. As Christians we have to know and study the word of God. We have to plant our lives in the Bible and allow it (our lives) to grow from the very pages of promises, instructions and blessings. We also should plant His word in our hearts and allow it (the word) to grow and produce a rich harvest of success in us. Remember what the Lord said:

> *The sky and the earth (the universe, the world) will pass away, but My words will not pass away.* [44]

The words of God carry an eternal value. It connects your life to eternity. It secures your future. When other things are stripped away through time or actions, and fade into the memory banks of history, the word of God remains fresh, potent, relevant and active. Within the pages of the Bible we find God's inspired will. He's given us every instruction, teaching and directive for Godly and successful living. It is imperative that we know and study the Bible. It remains the foundation and bedrock of our lives.

---

[44] Luke 21:33 AMP

So everyone who hears these words of Mine and acts upon them [obeying them] will be like a sensible (prudent, practical, wise) man who built his house upon the rock. And the rain fell and the floods came and the winds blew and beat against that house; yet it did not fall, because it had been founded on the rock. And everyone who hears these words of Mine and does not do them will be like a stupid (foolish) man who built his house upon the sand. And the rain fell and the floods came and the winds blew and beat against that house, and it fell — and great and complete was the fall of it. [45]

Prophecy

The Lord also communicates to us through prophetic utterance. Even here He can use a variety of ways to get His message across. He can use a messenger in the form of a prophetic voice. Or send someone your way with an encouraging word or prayer. It may even not be obvious or deliberate to you, as the Lord loves

---

[45] Matthew 7:24-27 AMP

41

to orchestrate scenes of our lives to tie in with destiny.

One day, Sharon was crossing a road in her hometown of Welkom in South Africa. There were a number of people crossing this busy street with her. She noticed a man walking right in front of her and became aware in her spirit that the Lord wanted her to go to this man and tell him: "Look up, the sun is shining." For some moments she struggled with this thought. After all she was in sunny South Africa were the sun seems to shine all the time! After some more prompting (or prodding) by the Holy Spirit, she walked up to this man and said: "Sir, the Lord wants me to tell you to look up because the sun is shining." Tears rushed to his eyes as peace flooded his soul. He told Sharon that his wife was battling cancer

> *Do not make important life choices based on prophecy alone.*

and just that morning he was feeling overwhelmed. His family was experiencing this dark cloud over them. He found himself asking the Lord if the sun will ever shine on their lives again. One simple sentence that made no sense to the messenger brought an amazing encouragement to a desperate man!

Throughout the Bible we find prophetic utterances as a valid way for the Lord to communicate to individuals as well as nations. It is important to note that messengers are fallible. The message may originate from the Lord but when filtered though someone's mind and heart can become distorted. The Lord did not make us to be gullible in our belief.

> *But the natural, non-spiritual man does not accept or welcome or admit into his heart the gifts and teachings and revelations of the Spirit of God, for they are folly (meaningless nonsense) to him; and he is incapable of knowing them [of progressively recognizing, understanding, and becoming better acquainted with them] because they are spiritually discerned and estimated and appreciated. But the spiritual man tries all things [he examines, investigates, inquires into, questions, and discerns all things],[46]*

All prophetic utterances to us or through us should be able to stand the test of the Word of

---

[46] 1 Corinthians 2:14 -15a AMP

God. Anything that goes against the grain of the Bible must be discarded. If it does not confirm what the Word of God already established in you then push it aside. Do not make important life choices based on prophecy alone.

> . . . *every word may be confirmed and upheld by the testimony of two or three witnesses.* [47]

We will turn our full attention to some aspects of the prophetic realm later in the book, but for now it is important to note that the Lord uses prophetic utterance as a valid way to communicate to people.

Angelic Visitation
Another way for God to communicate to people is through angelic messengers or visitations. Throughout the Bible we read of angels visiting people, sometimes with specific and detailed instructions and other times appearing without verbal instruction at all. (In Luke 2:13-14 the angels appeared to the shepherds and sang praises to God.) Remember angels are messengers and servants of God.

> *For He will give His angels [especial] charge over you to*

---

[47] Matthew 18:16b AMP

accompany and defend and preserve you in all your ways [of obedience and service]. They shall bear you up on their hands, lest you dash your foot against a stone. [48]

Even today the Lord still uses angels to accomplish His will. They can materialize in human form, visit you in your dreams, or remain unseen in the natural realm.

One day Sharon was sick in bed with a terrible infection. The doctor prescribed medication to her and after taking it she had an allergic reaction to it that nearly took her life. A friend was waiting at Sharon's bedside while I went into the study to pray. I was driven to pray. While I was praying I was caught up in a vision. It was as if I was standing in our bedroom looking at Sharon lying in bed. I saw what looked like a dark, shadowy figure busy choking my wife. I could not move. For a moment I felt helpless. I cried out to Jesus. "Lord, look at what this thing is doing to my wife!" Then suddenly two angels appeared in the room. One was big in stature and the second one smaller. They shimmered as the sun shone through the windows upon them. The big one

---

[48] Psalm 91:11-12 AMP

grabbed the dark shadowy demonic figure by the neck and back and carried him like a puppy-dog out of the room. The smaller angel was leading the way towards our back door. I followed in utter amazement. They stepped out onto our back porch and the big angel released the demon that immediately vanished into thin air. The two angels lingered in the sunlight for a few moments. They smiled and glistened, their appearance looked as if they were covered in golden glitter. Then they disappeared and I came out of the vision standing outside with Bullet, our trusted dog giving me a puzzled look.

I stepped back inside and went right to our bedroom where Sharon was. She was sitting up in bed. All the pain had left her body. She was sharing with her friend about the shadowy figure and the two angels that

> *The anchor in life that connects you to God and stretches through eternity is the Word of God.*

came to her rescue and how at that moment the Lord healed her. I was flabbergasted! We both had the same experience while it happened and her healing was proof that it really happened. After a good night's rest Sharon was back to her regular schedule with no infection or lingering fatigue at all! Praise God from whom all blessings flow!

Let me remind you again that the anchor in life that connects you to God and stretches through eternity is the Word of God. Should you experience an angelic visitation, always judge that experience, message or revelation within the context and "grain" of the Bible. If it does not agree with the essence of the Word, then God's not in it. The Bible warns us that Satan himself can *masquerade as an angel of light.*[49]

Visionary Experiences
What I described to you above came to us as a visionary experience. Visions and dreams are also valid ways for God to communicate to you. Did you know that over one third of all Bible verses deal with some or another visionary experience? Eschatology (the study of the End Times) is largely based upon the dreams and visions God gave people like Daniel, Ezekiel, Zachariah, John, Peter, Paul, etc. In a dream the Lord spoke to Solomon and imparted gifts to him that when he woke up he started to use his new understanding heart to judge the people of God.[50] Paul, instead of going to Bithynia as he originally planned, went to Macedonia to

---

[49] 2 Corinthians 11:14 AMP
[50] 1 Kings 3:5 AMP

preach the Gospel. This directional change in his ministry came because of a vision that he had.[51] Peter, while preparing for a meal, went into a trance and saw a vision that caused him to preach the Gospel of Jesus to Cornelius' household. This represented a significant cultural change for him, compelling him to share the Gospel of Jesus to Jews and Gentiles alike.[52] These are but a few examples of how the Lord might use dreams and visions to communicate to you.

> *And it shall come to pass in the last days,* **God declares, that I will pour out of My Spirit upon all mankind,** *and your sons and your daughters shall* **prophesy** *[telling forth the divine counsels] and your young men shall see* **visions** *(divinely granted appearances), and your old men shall dream [divinely suggested]* **dreams.**[53]

The Bible never warns us against visionary experiences. In fact, it is surprisingly positive towards them. It is our Western culture that embraced reason and logic to be the sole

---

[51] Acts 16:9 AMP
[52] Acts 10
[53] Acts 2:17 AMP Emphasis Added.

catalysts of knowledge and valid wisdom. Scripturally we can obtain knowledge, wisdom and direction through any of the ways God chooses to communicate to us. He is after all the Source of all knowledge and wisdom! Jesus gave us an excellent example:

> *So Jesus answered them by saying, I assure you, most solemnly I tell you, the Son is able to do nothing of Himself (of His own accord); but He is able to do only what He **sees** the Father doing, for whatever the Father does is what the Son does in the same way [in His turn].*[54]

Did you notice the present tense "sees" in this powerful verse? Jesus, at the time He uttered these words, was not in heaven with the Father. He was living His destiny here on earth, yet throughout His ministry He maintained a visionary link with what was current in the Throne Room of heaven. Whatever the Father was busy with in heaven, Jesus was doing on earth. Jesus would regularly go to great lengths to synchronize His life and ministry with the will of His Father in heaven. We should do the same. Whatever heaven is promoting today, we

---

[54] John 5:19 AMP Emphasis Added.

should busy ourselves with. What is fashionable there will be effective here. Stay current with the current flow of the Kingdom. One way to accomplish this synchronized life is through visionary experiences.

Revelations

The apostle Paul prayed a very powerful prayer in the book of Ephesians:

> *I do not cease to give thanks for you, making mention of you in my prayers. For I always pray to the God of our Lord Jesus Christ, the Father of glory, that He may grant you a* ***spirit of wisdom and revelation [of insight into mysteries and secrets] in the [deep and intimate] knowledge of Him,*** [55]

In this letter to the Ephesians he describes how the Lord has *lavished upon us every kind of wisdom and understanding (practical insight and prudence), making known to us the mystery (secret) of His will (of His plan, of His purpose).* [56] He then continues to pray for something even greater than what we had

---

[55] Ephesians 1:16 -17 AMP Emphasis Added.
[56] Ephesians 1:8 – 9 AMP

encountered before. Something that will enhance, exceed and amplify the lavished wisdom God already made available to us. A spirit of wisdom and revelation in the knowledge of Him! Our wisdom and understanding of things, people and circumstances is nothing without a spirit of wisdom and revelation in the knowledge Christ possesses. As Creator and Keeper of everything, God has intimate, correct and detailed knowledge of everything. We can tap into this vast reservoir of knowledge by getting to know Him in a deep and intimate way! We can connect to Him through a spirit of wisdom and

God is not a concealing God. He is revealing in His nature.

revelation. It has to be revealed to us, for we did not know such a tremendous depth before. We can know Him in ways we never knew before!

[Things are hidden temporarily only as a means to revelation.] For there is nothing hidden except to be revealed, nor is anything [temporarily] kept secret except in order that it may be made known.[57]

---

[57] Mark 4:24 AMP

Because of His infinite greatness, God seem to be enshrouded with mystery and surrounded by secrecy. Humanity's complexities cannot even challenge God's most rudimentary thoughts. What seems like wisdom to us is foolishness to God and He has chosen the foolish things of this world to put to shame the wise.[58] Yet God is not a concealing God. He is revealing in His nature. He loves to reveal secrets, to reveal things to you that you do not know.

> *Call to Me, and I will answer you,*
> *and show you great and mighty*
> *things, which you do not know.*[59]

The Lord has a way to reveal things to you. You may be reading a familiar verse in the Bible, when suddenly He opens a new truth and revelation to you. You might have been stumped with a certain problem, question or circumstance when suddenly you simply know what to do. What once has been so far above or beyond you now seem so near and within your grasp. That is the power of revelation.

Impressions
You will be impressed with God! Not that He always wants to impress people by showing off

---

[58] 1 Corinthians 1:27a
[59] Jeremiah 33:3 NKJV

His power, ability and wisdom or anything. He is impressive simply by being Who He is: Almighty God. One way He uses to communicate with you is through the impressions of the Holy Spirit. These are subtle promptings or nuances deep within you. Sometimes you will not be able to quite put your finger on it, or be able to describe in words what you sense He wants you to do. You will simply know to follow your heart in accordance with your spiritual senses. You can learn to obey these impressions through experience. Your spirit is a quick learner. Remember, everything starts with your knowledge of the inspired word of God. So study the word of God. Get it into your heart and it will also get into your head.

> *I APPEAL to you therefore, brethren, and beg of you in view of [all] the mercies of God, to make a decisive dedication of your bodies [presenting all your members and faculties] as a living sacrifice, holy (devoted, consecrated) and well pleasing to God, which is your reasonable (rational, intelligent) service and spiritual worship. Do not be conformed to this world (this age), [fashioned after and*

> *adapted to its external, superficial customs], but be transformed (changed) by the [entire] renewal of your mind [by its new ideals and its new attitude], so that you may prove [for yourselves] what is the good and acceptable and perfect will of God, even the thing which is good and acceptable and perfect [in His sight for you].[60]*

In your quest to know the will of God for your life, allow the transformational power of the word of God to renew your mind. Live your life according to the barometer of His word. *All who are led by the Spirit of God are sons of God.[61]*

Pictures

Pictures speak louder than words. It often takes a whole paragraph to aptly describe what a picture conveys. String many pictures together and you have a sequence of events, a storyline that captures the imagination. Jesus used pictures to communicate to His audience. He often spoke in metaphors and similes that made people understand even the most complex subject. *The kingdom of heaven is like a man who sowed good seed in his field. . .[62]* and *The*

---

[60] Romans 12:1-2 AMP
[61] Romans 8:14 AMP
[62] Matthew 13:24 AMP.

kingdom of heaven is like something precious buried in a field, which a man found and hid again; then in his joy he goes and sells all he has and buys that field. [63] *And, again, the kingdom of heaven is like a dragnet which was cast into the sea and gathered in fish of every sort.* [64]

The Kingdom of Heaven is more than a physical realm. It extends farther than the human heart can reach, and deeper than your mind can think. It is actively fluid, while invisibly stable, amazingly influential, and potently directional. It surpasses human endeavor and yet are within reach of even the simplest believer! Jesus described this Kingdom with word pictures in ways you and I can comprehend. The Lord also asked a specific question to prophets of old:

What do you see? [65]

Habakkuk said:

I will stand my watch and set myself on the rampart, and **watch to see what He will say to me,**

---

[63] Matthew 13:44 AMP.
[64] Matthew 13:47 AMP.
[65] Jeremiah 1:11, 1:13, 24:3; Amos 7:8, 8:2; Zech 4:2, 5:2 AMP

>*and what I will answer when I am corrected.*[66]

He did not say: "I will listen to the voice of the Lord." He said: "I will watch to see what the Lord will say to me." Do not merely dismiss the pictures in your mind and spirit. They can be messages from the Lord. Document these pictures. Ask the Lord to explain their meaning just like His disciples asked Him to explain the parable of the sower to them.[67] The Lord will draw on everyday things in your life to teach you concerning the things of the Spirit. Some of the greatest spiritual lessons come from the ordinary things that surround us.

Songs

Another wonderful way for the Lord to communicate to us is through song. Music

"He will exult over you with singing"

remains a universal heart language. Lyrics ride on the melody past normal barriers deep into the soul of a person. In meetings around the world the Lord would anoint Sharon and give her awesome spontaneous songs to sing over people. We call these God songs. With unique melodies and powerful lyrics that rhyme and

---

[66] Habakkuk 2:1 NKJV Emphasis Added
[67] Mark 4:10

flow with the music, the Lord would stir people's hearts. Many have been healed physically, emotionally and spiritually as a result. One Sunday night in Akron, Ohio the Lord gave Sharon a powerful song. The lyrics were simple, yet so powerful. "I belong to Jesus! I do not belong to anyone else but Jesus." As she sang the song the power of God came into the place. The front of the sanctuary filled up with people giving their hearts to Jesus. It was an awesome night of salvation, re-dedications and scores were marvelously filled with the Holy Spirit, all because of the song of the Lord!

> *The Lord your God is in the midst of you, a Mighty One, a Savior [Who saves]! He will rejoice over you with joy; He will rest [in silent satisfaction] and in His love He will be silent and make no mention [of past sins, or even recall them];* ***He will exult over you with singing.*** [68]

The Hebrew word translated "exult" here means "properly, to spin around (under the influence of any violent emotion), i.e. usually rejoice, to

---

[68] Zephaniah 3:17 AMP. Emphasis added.

be glad, joy, be joyful."[69] Can you imagine Almighty God catching a glimpse of you, being so stirred with emotion in His heart that He spins around, rejoicing and singing a song over you? Wow, in the words of Crush, that lovable hippy-sea-turtle in Disney's Finding Nemo: "Totally awesome dude!"

The apostle Paul also linked singing as a way the Holy Spirit would work in the hearts of God's people.

> *And do not get drunk with wine, for that is debauchery; but ever be filled and stimulated with the [Holy] Spirit. Speak out to one another in psalms and hymns and spiritual songs, offering praise with voices [and instruments] and making melody with all your heart to the Lord,*[70]

Psalms here are scripture songs i.e. Psalms of David set to music. Hymns here are songs that bring glory to God through human expression. Spiritual songs here are spontaneous God songs directly inspired by the Holy Spirit. So sing a new song unto the Lord! Go ahead and let your

---

[69] Strong's Dictionary of Bible words Hebrew #1523
[70] Ephesians 5:18 – 19 AMP.

spirit man sing as the Holy Spirit composes beautiful songs that will glorify God and edify your heart.

> *He has put a new song in my mouth, a song of praise to our God.*[71]

Inner voice

You have a built in ability to sense God's inner voice, also known as *the still, small voice*[72]. In fact, there is nothing small about it! It carries the same power and potential as the loudest shout from heaven. The prophet Elijah was

Even when the Lord speaks to you when no one else is listening, it can be monumental in your life

exposed to a variety of ways the Lord communicated to him. Whether through fire from Heaven or deep intercession for rain, he heard from God. This time the Lord spoke to Him in a still, small voice and asked him: *"What are you doing here, Elijah?"* Through the still, small voice the Lord instructed Elijah to do some pretty loud and enormous things. He was to anoint a new king over Syria, a new king

---

[71] Psalm 40:3a AMP.
[72] 1 Kings 19:12 – 13 AMP

over Israel, a new prophet in his place. These are amazingly strategic directional changes that would affect nations and territories, shaping destinies for future generations to come. All that from a still, small voice! Wow! Do you share my need to hear God speak in this manner? Even when the Lord speaks to you when no one else is listening, it can be monumental in your life! Those God-whispers often will impact your life in a dramatic way.

Audible voice
God's voice can come to you audibly. My experience has been that most often it is not audible, though we must know that He can make His voice heard in the realm of the natural. Too many people, I fear are waiting and straining their natural ears to hear the audible voice of the Lord. They expect a deep authoritative voice that makes all resistance crumble at the sound of it. The Lord certainly has captured the attention of people in this way before and He will likely do it again.

You will do well however to position your life to receive all the ways He wants to communicate to you. Do not eliminate any one of these valid ways of divine communication simply to hope for a more spectacular or powerful experience. God's whispers are just as potent and life-changing! It is not the vehicle that carries the contents that is to be admired. It is context of what God wants to say to you that needs attention. Zero in on the message and be thankful for the variety of messengers He employs to get the job done. If you are diligent you will become aware of Him communicating to you all the time! It could be in any or all of the ways I described in this chapter. It might even be through a sermon, or teaching, a poem or a book like this one. You may sit on the beach with your toes in the sand and He might "speak" to you through the waves rolling in with the tide. You may sit at you desk when suddenly the screen of your heart captures a picture from Heaven.

Position your life in such a way that it will welcome, observe and cherish God's communications with you.

CHAPTER 3
YOUR SPIRITUAL SENSES

The Lord blessed your natural body with five natural senses. Of course many people would add a sixth sense to the adornment of the fairer sex, but allow me to focus for a moment on those five natural senses. They are your sense of sight, your sense of hearing, your sense of taste, your sense of smell and your sense of feeling.

Your body is truly amazing! Every one of your senses is connected to your central nervous (processing) center, and to your brain. They cannot function without this attachment. In fact your brain controls their function. Perfectly good eyes must be connected to a functioning brain that can process the images you are looking at.

I believe that just as your five natural senses are your body's way of interacting with your natural environment, so too the Lord gave you five spiritual senses to interact with the realm of the spirit and ultimately with God. What we have in the natural is a mere reflection of a more potent spiritual configuration.

Sense of Seeing

I cannot even begin to describe all the features and processes it takes to cause you to see naturally. Your eye is self-focusing. When you look at something close to you, a word on the page of this book, or gaze across towards your horizon, your eyes automatically adjusts your focus. A malfunction in your ability to focus calls for corrective measures; you may need glasses or contacts, or even surgery. Without focus, sight is blurred and not useful at all.

You have spiritual sight. Physiologically your eyes are located near the highest place on your body. This placement is strategic in that it gives you the best possible vantage point for increased vision. Spiritually your eyes are also strategically placed. They are connected to your spirit to afford you the best possible sight. But sight alone is not useful at all. Your spiritual sight must be combined with spiritual focus. Many simply gaze into the spiritual realm, some using a variety of

> *You spiritual eyes give you the ability to see things close to your heart.*

methods, hoping to spot something they can make out and comprehend. Correct and automatic focus to your spiritual eyes will only come when your spirit is connected to the Holy Spirit. His function as it pertains to your spiritual sight is much like your brain in connection with your eyes. Your spirit will see things, but the Holy Spirit will bring focus, color, dimension, insight, clarity and perception to it.

You spiritual eyes give you the ability to see things close to your heart. It reveals spiritual insight to things you are within reach of. It also allows for destiny vision, a tremendous ability to see the potent potential the Lord has prepared for you and placed on the horizon of the next seasons of your life. If you can perceive them, you can position your life according to those phenomenal plans of God for your life! Spiritual eyes are neither near nor far sighted. Spiritual insight will balance immediate priorities with future destinies. As you develop and exercise your spiritual eyes you will have hindsight, insight, and foresight. You'll have the ability to look back and learn from things gone by. Your will be able to process, respond to, and understand things presently present in your life. You will also be able to anticipate, cherish and perceive things that are to come.

> *[For I always pray to] the God of our Lord Jesus Christ, the Father of glory, that He may grant you a spirit of wisdom and revelation [of insight into mysteries and secrets] in the [deep and intimate] knowledge of Him, **By having the eyes of your heart flooded with light**, so that you can know and understand the hope to which He has called you, and how rich is His glorious inheritance in the saints (His set-apart ones), [73]*

What a powerful prayer! You can have the spirit of wisdom and revelation in the knowledge of Jesus by having the eyes of your heart flooded with light. That will also allow you to understand the hope He has called you to and the glorious inheritance He bestowed upon you as a follower of Christ!

Eyes also have blind spots, areas where sight is blurred or hidden away. Have you ever looked into the side mirror of your vehicle to see if it is clear to change lanes on the highway? You looked, saw no traffic and started towards the lane next to you. Then, suddenly and slightly behind your line of sight appeared a car with a

---

[73] Ephesians 1:17-18 AMP. Emphasis Added.

loud horn that warned your brain to override the "clear" message from your eyes. That car was in your blind spot.

That makes me wonder how many significant things are in our blind spots spiritually!

> *Therefore I counsel you to purchase from Me gold refined and tested by fire, that you may be [truly] wealthy, and white clothes to clothe you and to keep the shame of your nudity from being seen, **and salve to put on your eyes, that you may see.***[74]

We will do well to make sure we are constantly checking, looking, watching to see what the Lord is doing around us. He is the One to open our eyes to see.

> *Then their eyes were opened and they knew Him; and He vanished from their sight.*[75]

The two men from Emmaus were actually walking and talking with Jesus. They were believers that committed and devoted their lives

---

[74] Revelations 3:18 AMP. Emphasis Added.
[75] Luke 24:31 NKJV

to the Lord. Yet in those defining moments when He graced their lives with His personal and intimate presence, they never saw that it was Him! Only when the Lord opened their eyes they realized that it was Him! May the Lord open our eyes as well! May we see Him in His splendor walking and talking with us too!

Have you ever wondered why the Lord blessed people with two eyes instead on one? No your other eye is not a spare! When you look through one eye you can see detail, color, movement, etc. But you loose a very important dimension of vision: depth perception. With one eye it becomes near impossible to calculate distance. One eye vision is two dimensional. With two eyes you see 3D! You can perceive depth and distance. Scripturally spiritual eyes are referred to in the plural. Your spiritual eyes can calculate distance and depth. Your spiritual sight is multi-dimensional and receives the revelations of the Lord in the vibrant full colors of life! Do not be spiritually color blind! Remember, the word of God is a great visual aid (spectacles, glasses) to fully see His revelation. Look through the glasses of the

> *Your spiritual sight is multi-dimensional and receives the revelations of the Lord in the vibrant full colors of life!*

word and you will see things crisp and clear, in high definition and with deep insights.

Sense of Hearing

Your ears detect sounds. *Sound is a form of energy that moves through water, air and other matter in waves of pressure. Sound waves are perceived by the brain through the firing of nerve cells in the auditory portion of the central nervous system. The ear changes sound pressure waves from the outside world into a signal of nerve impulses sent to the brain.*[76]

As with your eye, your ears function properly when connected to your brain. It is your brain that "decodes" the sounds detected by your ears. It is important to note that not all sounds are audible, detectable by your ears. Audible sounds fall within a rather small frequency range. Just because your biological ears does not detect these sounds, does not mean that the sounds does not exist. Think of a dog whistle. Its full sound is silent to your ears, but your dog hears it very well and responds accordingly.

> *But he who enters by the door is the shepherd of the sheep. To him the doorkeeper opens, **and the sheep hear his voice**; and he calls*

---

[76] http://en.wikipedia.org/wiki/Ear

his own sheep by name and leads them out.[77]

The Lord placed in your spirit the capacity to "hear" the sound of His Shepherd-voice along with the sounds coming from heaven. They resonate in the hearts of the believers who is tuned into the frequency of heaven. Whenever God does something it releases tremendous amounts of energy. He said: "Let there be light. And there was light." It came to being because of the sounds emanating from His mouth. Sound waves are energy! We have already determined that heaven is not a quiet place. Worship sounds like thunder.

> *And I heard a voice from heaven like the sound of great waters and like the rumbling of mighty thunder; the voice I heard [seemed like the music] of harpists accompanying themselves on their harps. And they sang a new song before the throne [of God]*[78]

The voices of angels declaring the holiness of the Lord make the foundations of the thresholds

---

70

of heaven shake.[79] Add to that the voice of the Lord as we discussed in chapter 1 of this book! Indeed, when you think of heaven please do not think of it in terms of an empty cathedral-like place with soft religious organ music, some candles for atmosphere, with a few gatherings scheduled every now and then. Wherever life is, sound and noise is generated! What I want you to realize is that you have access to these sounds. You are able to hear and detect what the Lord says in the throne room of heaven and what He whispers in your heart.

Another amazing characteristic of hearing is that it never stops. Even when you sleep, your ears are always working! That's why the most effective alarm to wake you in the morning does so with sound. Your ears never get tired to listen. They are on their post 24/7! I love this feature. Similarly, your spirit has the ability to pick up the voice and sounds from heaven all the time. You do not have to be oblivious to what is going on around you, especially in the realm of the spirit. Listen past the static and noise of the natural realm, and tune into the frequency of the Holy Spirit. Go ahead and practice to hear His voice and to listen by obeying that voice. Do not wait for audible instructions. Employ the use of your spirit more

---

[79] Isaiah 6:4

than your biological ears. Every time I preach the word of God, I do my very best to keep my ears tuned towards heaven. My spirit will regularly pick up directions and instructions "on the fly" that, when delivered, impact people in a powerful way. We have seen meetings bust open spiritually and thrust people to new heights of spiritual experience simply because we listened to God's instruction for those specific times.

I always say to people that the Lord has given us two ears and one mouth for good reason. We are to listen twice as much as we speak. Make time everyday to listen with your heart. Creative opportunities to fine tune your spirit to pick up and register the spiritual sounds around you. I believe you can actually increase your spiritual hearing through practice, faith and obedience.

> *So faith comes by hearing [what is told], and what is heard comes by the preaching [of the message that came from the lips] of Christ (the Messiah Himself).* [80]

It is interesting to note that the Bible connects your faith with your ability to hear! When you hear the declared word or message of God your

---

[80] Romans 10:17 AMP

faith is activated. This is an important reason why I love to read the Bible aloud. Speaking it is a tremendous blessing because the word of God in your mouth is just as powerful as the word of God in His mouth! Hearing it adds to that blessing by producing, stirring, and activating faith with which you can please God, move mountains, and so much more. Your whole being will respond at hearing the voice and instructions of the Lord.

Sense of Feeling
Your skin is your largest organ. It covers every part of your body. It is equipped with millions of nerve endings, sensors and the like that receives stimuli in a variety of ways. Your skin is also connected to your brain via a collaborative nervous system. Your skin is sensitive to touch, detects pain and has strong connections to your emotions.

Feelings can be your friend of foe. When you rely on feeling as your dominant sense in life, *Feelings can be your friend of foe.* your world will be "topsy-turvy". Feeling is not an enduring or lasting expression. As soon as the stimulus that caused a certain feeling is removed, then that specific feeling will cease. As believers we are to pay attention to our spiritual sense of awareness and discernment.

The Lord made available to us the ability to "try" all things.

> *But the natural, non-spiritual man does not accept or welcome or admit into his heart the gifts and teachings and revelations of the Spirit of God, for they are folly (meaningless nonsense) to him; and he is incapable of knowing them [of progressively recognizing, understanding, and becoming better acquainted with them]* **because they are spiritually discerned and estimated and appreciated. But the spiritual man tries all things [he examines, investigates, inquires into, questions, and discerns all things]**[81]

When you develop your spiritual ability to discern things; to recognize given situations with the aid of the Holy Spirit; when you see through the many layers of pretense anything may be covered with, then this sense becomes a valuable ally in life. It keeps you sober without being suspicious. It stirs aptitude in the absence of a harmful attitude. It releases the tangible

---

[81] 1 Corinthians 2:14 – 15a AMP

anointing and presence of God into any given situation. Too many of God's precious people have been gullible before, being swayed emotionally to act, or make important decisions. The Lord has provided for you with a spiritual awareness when amplified by the gift of the *discerning of spirits*[82] will reinforce your stance in life. It will allow you to soar above situations and never become a product of circumstances.

Your spiritual awareness can be numbed in a variety of ways. Sin in general acts as a Novocain of sorts that renders your discernment useless for a season. You will not detect spiritual attacks, evil intrusions, divine visitations, etc. We should never tolerate sin of any kind in our lives. When we sinned, we should confess our sin to keep our hearts pure before God and keep our lives protected.

Applications and Functions of Spiritual Awareness

Your skin has a number of functions. It protects you from intrusion and infections. Your spiritual sense of discernment also protects you from spiritual infections like sin, compromise, etc.

---

[82] 1 Corinthians 12:10

Sensation is also a function of your skin. Spiritually you can get a sense of things around you. You can pick up the atmosphere in a room, the mood of a person or an opportunity the Lord brings your way.

Your skin regulates the heat of your body. It acts as your biological thermometer. I believe the Lord has given you the spiritual ability to not only be a thermometer, but a thermostat. A thermostat regulates the temperature in a room while the thermometer only measures it. You can change the spiritual atmosphere wherever you go. You can regulate the spiritual climate around you!

Your skin controls evaporation. Spiritually you want to have a handle on the process of spiritual evaporation. Have you ever received a tremendous blessing from God in a meeting at church on Sunday only to wonder on Tuesday where that power has gone? It is as if it evaporated from your spirit. This sense of spiritual awareness will allow you to gauge the rate of spiritual evaporation, slowing it down and even warn you to replenish your spiritual substance before you run dry.

Your skin is a powerful communicator. A tender caress, a hard shove, even a chill down your spine sends clear wordless messages.

When your spiritual discernment is operating like it should, you will feel the love of God, sense His touch and anticipate His will for your life. You'll be aware of His presence without words or feeling. You'll just know.

Your skin stores water and absorbs among other things, medications. Your spiritual discernment will likewise retain crucial reserves of the word of God (likened to water is Ephesians 5:26). It will also absorb powerful spiritual medications, balms, oils, and remedies into your being to heal, strengthen and protect you from hurt, trauma, sickness and weakness. Your skin excretes toxins in the form of sweat. In fact, medical professionals place a high value on a good sweat during and after exercise. Your spirit has the ability to release toxins that contaminate your mind, emotions and perspectives. Like sweat through the pores of your skin, your spirit will cause these contaminants to flow from you.

You will do well to recognize and develop this wonderful spiritual sense of discernment and awareness He has placed in you.

Sense of Smell
Your nose is not a mere facial adornment or annoyance when you look in the mirror. It has a very powerful function. It captures aromatic

smells and relays them to your brain for processing. *There are a number of theories that endeavor to explain olfactory perception or the sense of smell. None can do so completely due to the complex nature of the smelling process.*[83] *Biologically you have been equipped with about 40 million olfactory receptor neurons. Through a series of complex processes these recognize and bind with odor molecules resulting in smell.*[84]

Did you know that spiritually you also have the ability to smell? There is an aroma connected to worship and prayer. Heaven is a fragrant place.

> *And another angel came and stood over the altar. He had a golden censer, and he was given* **very much incense (fragrant spices and gums which exhale perfume when burned), that he might mingle it with the prayers of all the people of God** *(the saints) upon the golden altar before the throne. [Ps 141:2.] And* **the smoke of the incense (the perfume) arose in the presence of God**, *with the prayers of the*

---

[83] http://en.wikipedia.org/wiki/Olfaction
[84] http://en.wikipedia.org/wiki/Olfactory_receptor_neuron

people of God (the saints), from the hand of the angel.[85]

Your spiritual life carries a potent fragrance. Even the knowledge of God has a fragrance.

*But thanks be to God, Who in Christ always leads us in triumph [as trophies of Christ's victory] and through us spreads and makes evident **the fragrance of the knowledge of God everywhere**, for we are the **sweet fragrance of Christ** [which exhales] unto God, [discernible alike] among those who are being saved and among those who are perishing.*[86]

One of the great characteristics about the sense of smell is that it is connected to life-memories. When you smell a specific smell it can stir memories in you of where you had been when you smelt it before.

Spiritually you can be stimulated in the presence of God or the atmosphere of heaven.

These memories can

---

[85] Revelation 8:3-4 AMP. Emphasis Added.
[86] 2 Corinthians 2:14-15 AMP. Emphasis Added.

be sweet or bitter, good or bad. Whenever I smell the perfume Sharon wore when we first met many years ago, it takes me back to wonderful memories of the blossoming love between us. Spiritually you can be stimulated in the presence of God or the atmosphere of heaven. Memories of spiritual experiences such as salvation or being filled with the Holy Spirit are powerful reminders of God's power in your life.

Smell recognizes and identifies food. Spiritually you can identify what will satisfy you spirit. Jesus is called the Bread of Life. Have you ever smelled the fragrance of fresh baked bread? During our first year of marriage we stayed in an apartment directly above a bakery. Every morning around 6 AM we would wake up to the insistent smell of bread, begging us to go from smelling to tasting. The flavor of food is not just tasted. It is smelled too. When your spiritual sense of smell is developed you'll be able to recognize the various flavors of worship, prayer, intercession and blessing.

There is another type of smell that will possibly give a great illustration of your spiritual sense of smell. Scientists have discovered substances called pheromones. These are unconscious odor cues. They are smelled unconsciously; the smeller may not even be aware of their smell yet be stimulated by them. There are a slew of different types of these pheromones. Alarm pheromones trigger flight or aggression in bees. Trail pheromones are used by ants to mark their paths. Territorial pheromones are in the urine of dogs to mark their claimed territories. Consider the possibility of spiritual stimuli, undetectable in the realm of the natural but highly potent in the realm of the Spirit, activated by a spiritual sense comparable to your sense of smell.

Be full of love for others, following the example of Christ who loved you and gave himself to God as a sacrifice to take away your sins. And God was pleased, **for Christ's love for you was like sweet perfume to him.** [87]

Here the love of Christ is expressed as a sweet perfume. If it is like a sweet perfume to the Father then surely we can "smell" it too and be stimulated by His amazing love!

Mary expressed her love and devotion to Jesus by pouring a pound of expensive pure nard (a rare perfume) on Jesus' feet and wiping them with her hair. The Bibles declares that the

---

[87] Ephesians 5:2 TLB Emphasis Added.

whole house where Jesus was was filled with the fragrance of the perfume.[88]

Allow me to ask you a provocative question. If indeed your life could be captured as a smell in the nostrils of God, what would that smell be like to Him? Would it be pleasing to Him or repulsive? Would the smell of your life take Him back to those beautiful, intimate times with you in His presence? Would He want to linger around you like someone in complete appreciation of a rose garden in full bloom? Or would your life smell like a garbage dump on the outskirts of a filthy city?

Sense of Taste

> *O taste and see that the Lord [our God] is good!*[89]

The proof of the pudding is in the eating! Your sense of taste partners with your sense of smell to detect flavor of food. Taste is also a function of your central nervous system. It is said that you have 4 basic tastes: sweetness, sourness, bitterness and saltiness.

[88] John 12:3
[89] Psalm 34:8 AMP.

Spiritually you have the ability to taste. You can develop this spiritual palette into that of a connoisseur or "super-taster"!

> *How sweet are Your words to my taste, sweeter than honey to my mouth! [Ps 19:10; Prov 8:11.]*[90]

I am somewhat of a stickler when it comes to tasting new foods. I am quite happy to stick with what I am familiar with because when I taste something that I do not like, my appetite heads home long before me. My wife, Sharon on the other hand, is an adventurer when it comes to food. She loves to taste new and even exotic foods. So when we are in company and I'm served with something I find questionable, I'll ask her in our native language: "Honey will I like this?"

A powerful way to activate and develop your spiritual sense of taste is to stir your hunger for God

After many years of blissful marriage, she knows me well enough to know what type of taste I would like. Friend, God knows me even better! And He knows you too. He made us. When He prepares a table in the presence of our

---

[90] Psalm 118:103 AMP.

enemies[91], He is not going to load that table with foods we abhor and tastes we hate. When He prepares what eye has not seen and what ears have not heard and what has not entered the hearts of man, simply because of love[92], then you have to know that it will leave a pleasant taste in your mouth.

Taste is connected to satisfaction. Jesus said:

> *What father among you, if his son asks for a loaf of bread, will give him a stone; or if he asks for a fish, will instead of a fish give him a serpent? Or if he asks for an egg, will give him a scorpion? If you then, evil as you are, know how to give good gifts [gifts that are to their advantage] to your children, how much more will your heavenly Father give the Holy Spirit to those who ask and continue to ask Him![93]*

Note that the examples the Lord uses here are all edible, bread, fish and egg. Some may ask for bread, others for a fish and yet others for an egg. It depends on your palette or appetite.

---

[91] Psalm 23:5
[92] 1 Corinthians 2:9
[93] Luke 11:11-13 AMP.

Notice how the Holy Spirit can fulfill all your wants, needs and desires!

You sense of taste is always amplified with hunger. I grew up with a saying in South Africa: When the cat is full the mouse is bitter! Food does not taste nearly as good if you are not hungry. A powerful way to activate and develop your spiritual sense of taste is to stir your hunger for God.

> *For He satisfies the longing soul and fills the hungry soul with good.*[94]

Develop a taste for righteousness (right standing with God). And you will be fully satisfied.[95] Acquire a taste for spiritual food and you'll feast at the Lord's Table everyday!

---

[94] Psalm 107:9 AMP.
[95] Matthew 5:6

CHAPTER 4
POSITIONED. . .
to HEAR the VOICE OF the LORD

"So, Rudi given all the facts about the voice of the Lord, its characteristics, variety and my spiritual senses, how do I hear His voice?" Let's start to answer that question in this chapter!

To hear any voice you have to be within hearing distance. To hear the voice of the Lord regularly you have to be tuned into His divine frequency. He has the ability to catch your attention even when you are out and about your own business. Many people, who lived their lives far removed from a loving relationship with God, have been jerked back to the divine reality by some godly intervention. The Lord has a way of grabbing someone's attention as an extreme measure to rescue that person, often from themselves. These are life-changing grace moments.

But the purpose of this book is to teach you to communicate with the Lord and to hear His voice intelligently **all the time**. We are in pursuit of a deliberate experience and not just a random intervention. To accomplish this we have to be tuned in to heaven while clearing out all the outside noises. Clarity is determined and dependent on a few things:

Obedience
Have you obeyed the word of God to the best of your ability as he has revealed it to you?

> *Your word is a lamp to my feet and a light to my path.* [96]

Remember to position your life towards the word of God. Study it and the direction and path of you life will be illuminated.

> *But He said, Blessed (happy and to be envied) rather are those who hear the Word of God and obey and practice it!* [97]

There are many scriptural rewards for obedience. In fact the Lord places a very high priority to obey His voice. It brings all kinds of

---

[96] Psalm 119:105 AMP
[97] Luke 11:28 AMP

blessings into your life. The list is too long to mention here. You might want to cross reference the word "obey" in your concordance or Bible software.

> *But be doers of the Word [obey the message], and not merely listeners to it, betraying yourselves [into deception by reasoning contrary to the Truth].* [98]

When the Lord places something in your heart to do just do it. Go ahead and get it done. It does not matter how insignificant it may be. One day I was driving to our home after a long day at the office. While waiting for the traffic light to turn green, the Holy Spirit prompted me to turn at the next intersection. There was no scheduled turn on my way home. A turn would not lead me home. I turned simply because I wanted to obey that inner prompting. I had no idea where the Lord was going to take me. After I made the turn I said: "Ok Lord, where to now?" He said: "Go home son, I wanted you to practice hearing my voice." Wow! I cannot even begin to explain to you the sense of peace and joy that settled in my spirit because of a simple act of obedience. True, in the grand

---

[98] James 1:22 AMP

scope of life, that turn was insignificant and some will even consider it a waste of my time. But to me it was a lesson on how to hear the voice of the Lord. Next time that voice comes to me, regardless of the form it comes in, I would have a reference to fall back onto saying: "Hey, I know that voice. Last time I listened and obeyed I was rewarded with a deep peace and bubbling joy." Do you think I will be inclined to listen again? Absolutely! Next time may even be something more than a simple turn. It could save a life or prevent a gross mistake.

> *And we receive from Him whatever we ask, because we [watchfully] obey His orders [observe His suggestions and injunctions, follow His plan for us] and [habitually] practice what is pleasing to Him.*[99]

What do you do when you are in a season of seeming silence; when God's voice is somehow alarmingly quiet in your life? Obey His written word and continue to observe His last instruction to you. My

> **Your spirit connects you to God. It is the God-portion in you.**

---

[99] John 3:55 AMP

experience is that few things will stir the Lord to activate His voice over your life like obedience.

Focus on the Spirit

We are spirit beings. In fact you are a spirit, you have a soul and you live in a body. Your life should touch all three areas. Your body keeps your feet on the ground here in the realm of the natural. You soul houses your emotions, intellect, etc. The soul-realm plays an important part in your everyday existence. Your spirit connects you to God. It is the God-portion in you. This is also the place where you will receive God's communications.

> *But you are not living the life of the flesh, you are living the life of the Spirit, if the [Holy] Spirit of God [really] dwells within you [directs and controls you].*[100]

You have to learn to live life in the Spirit.[101] You have to focus your attention and affection towards the Spirit. You have to fix your eyes on Jesus, the Author and Finisher of your faith.[102] And you have to have the mind of Christ and hold the thoughts, feelings and purposes of His

---

[100] Romans 8:9 AMP.
[101] Galatians 5:25
[102] Hebrews 12:2

heart.[103] These are all disciplines that will ensure your posture and positioning before the Lord.

You will hear the voice of the Lord much more frequently and clearly in the realm of the spirit than waiting for a word in the realm of the flesh. If you rely too strong on the realm of your soul with its emotional interferences and intellectual reasoning the voice of God will be muted or muffled in the presence of all that "soul-noise". No, rather get Heaven's download in your spirit. Pay attention to it, document it and then apply it to the other realms of your life.

Trust in God

Trust is born out of relational experience. People trust people they know. Your spiritual trust-level will soar as your relationship with God develops. Pretty soon you'll know that He is completely reliable, utterly trustworthy, void of any shortcomings and perfect in every way. When you look at the character of God, with such attributes and actions you'll find it easy to trust Him.

This trust is important to clearly hear what He is saying to you. You'll be able to hear His heart

---

[103] 1 Corinthians 2:16 AMP.

and not just His words. You will not have to scrutinize His motives and judge His requests. Your trust in Him will open wide the channels of communication. It will allow Him to talk to you in a way a Father will talk to His child, or as good friends speak to each other.[104]

Take time to listen

Have you ever spoken to someone who was doing a bunch of other stuff at the same time? One day I was watching rugby on TV. My favorite teams were playing and the game was really intense. Sharon came to me to ask me a question. It was so difficult to pull my attention away from the screen. Somehow me ears heard the words that came from her mouth, but my heart was not listening. I was not able to answer her, not because I did not hear her words, but because I did not listen to them.

You want to hear the words that the Lord will speak to you as well as listen to them. Hearing is just a part of the experience. What are you doing to listen? You will do well to set time apart simply to listen; to process your hearing. Listening almost implies obedience, or at least the start of it. Listening takes more time, greater focus and determined attention than hearing.

---

[104] Ephesians 2:19; Galatians 4:7

Create listening times in your schedule. Make time for it.

> *Making the very most of the time [buying up each opportunity], because the days are evil.*[105]

Tune in

Another way to ensure clarity when hearing the voice of the Lord is best described as fine-tuning a radio to a preferred station. Nowadays most radios come with pre-set channels. You select a station and the frequency is automatically adjusted. Every radio however still has a tuning button. It is used to pinpoint the signal frequency. We recently installed a satellite dish. We had to aim the dish in the right direction to get the strongest possible signal. Do you get the point? Your spiritual antennas must be directed to and tuned towards the frequency of the Holy Spirit to "pick up" the voice of the Lord with clarity. The common radio band has many frequency positions to accommodate a slew of stations. Similarly, there are many voices you can tune to in order to get your life's direction from. God's voice is on a spiritual frequency unlike any of the other voices.

---

[105] Ephesians 5:16 AMP.

> *And since this great High Priest of ours rules over God's household,* **let us go right in to God himself,** *with true hearts fully trusting him to receive us because we have been sprinkled with Christ's blood to make us clean and because our bodies have been washed with pure water.*[106]

You can go right to God. You can draw near and be within hearing distance. Do not stay at a distance. You have an invitation. Draw near to God and He will draw near to you; closer means clearer. Let us look at this powerful verse closer to see what you can do to fine-tune your spirit to hear from the Lord.

True or clean hearts

You must ensure a clean heart in order to come near to the Lord. The Psalmist said only those with pure hearts and

A true heart comes near to God to learn and to love

clean hands can ascend to the mountain of God or stand in His Holy Place.[107] We are to guard our hearts above all for out of it flows the issues

---

[106] Hebrews 10:21-22 TLB Emphasis Added.
[107] Psalm 24:4

of life.[108] A pure heart is attained only through repentance and forgiveness. You repent and God forgives. A true heart comes near to God to learn and to love. It is filled with genuine trust and reliance on Him.

Absolute conviction by faith

Faith pleases God. Fill your heart with faith before it can be filled with anything else. You do not come to God unsure and in a tentative way. After your heart is purified and filled with the word of God, your faith takes flight, lifting you above circumstance, fear, and unbelief. Now you can approach the throne of grace fearlessly, confidently and boldly.[109]

Hearts sprinkled from a guilty conscience.

Your conscience is the voice of your spirit. Every human being was given a conscience to help them navigate between right and wrong. Those who yield to their conscience will live life in the right, pulling happiness, joy and fulfillment into their existence. Those who ignore their conscience actually sear it.[110] It becomes immobilized in their lives. They lose their ability to perceive right from wrong. The divine order of life is replaced with a self

---

[108] Proverbs 4:23
[109] Hebrews 4:16 AMP.
[110] 1 Timothy 4:2

centered, humanistic "whatever-feels-right-for-me" take on life and leads to eternal destruction.

Your conscience is one of your greatest allies. It is like a build-in navigational system that keeps you headed in the right direction. It does need regular maintenance though. When you apply the precious blood of Jesus to your life, it is sprinkled on your heart and thus cleans, maintains and re-calibrates your conscience. The blood of Jesus cleanses you of all sin and guilt when you live in fellowship with the Light (Jesus).[111] A sprinkled heart gives you the ability to draw near to Him because your conscience is in working order free from guilt and shame.

Body cleansed with pure water
Another way to fine-tune your spirit to draw near to God is to have your body washed and cleansed with pure water. This is a powerful word picture. Have you ever stepped into a warm, relaxing shower or bath after a long day's work? Of course you have! Stepping in is one thing, but stepping out is really what you are after. Than clean, fresh feeling! All the day's dirt, sweat and grime is washed away leaving you refreshed and smelling like a million dollars! Your significant other now can

---

[111] 1 John 1:17

come close to you without holding his or her breath.

The word of God is described as water in the book of Ephesians.

> *So that He might sanctify her, having **cleansed her by the washing of water with the Word**,*
> 112

Our verse in Hebrews 10 speaks of this as well. The word of God cleanses our bodies. It is interesting to note the target areas of the blood of Jesus and word of God. The blood targets our hearts to eliminate guilt from our conscience. The word of God targets our hearts, working its way through our whole body to cleanse us.

This four-way action of having true hearts, resolute faith, hearts sprinkled from a guilty conscience and our bodies cleansed with pure water afford us the ability to draw near to God; to step into hearing distance of His voice.

Habakkuk, a prophet who belonged to the tribe of Levi, was officially qualified to take part in the liturgical singing of the Temple.[113] He lived

---

[112] Ephesians 5:26 AMP. Emphasis Added.
[113] New Unger's Bible Dictionary

in a period of Chaldean cruelty on the people of God. Their life circumstances were not the best. He desperately needed a word from the Lord pronto; after all he was known to be a prophet.

> *[OH, I know, I have been rash to talk out plainly this way to God!] I will [in my thinking] stand upon my post of observation and station myself on the tower or fortress, and will watch to see what He will say within me and what answer I will make [as His mouthpiece] to the perplexities of my complaint against Him. And the Lord answered me and said, Write the vision and engrave it so plainly upon tablets that everyone who passes may [be able to] read [it easily and quickly] as he hastens by.*[114]

Look what he did to hear to hear the voice of God:

"I will stand my watch"
He sets himself as a watchman. Back then a watchman was an "out-looker" and a "careful watcher", even a "defender or guarder". He

---

[114] Habakkuk 2:1-2 AMP

would station himself on a strategic vantage point and watch for anything that would enter his view. Today, if you want to hear the voice of the Lord you should follow Habakkuk's example. Be a watchman. Be on the lookout for anything the Lord would bring into your spiritual view. Be a careful watcher and an out-looker. Be a defender of the word of God, guarding it in your heart at all times. Open your spirit to receive revelation from the Lord.

"I will station myself on the tower"

The next thing Habakkuk did was to position him strategically to receive revelation from the Lord. He stationed himself on the tower of observation. He found a place that is conducive to see; a place with few hindrances and distractions. A place with a spiritual view! He went where he could be alone and able to focus all his attention on hearing from the Lord. This is a very important point. Position yourself deliberately to hear from the Lord. Find a place of observation. Some people like to drive up a mountain to pray. Others go for a walk on the beach. Yet, others find a quiet place in their homes and designate time to commune with the Lord. Some get up early in the morning when all is quiet around

> *Position yourself deliberately to hear from the Lord.*

them. Others stay up late at night when loved ones have retired to bed. Some business people spend their lunch hour on a park bench seeking the Lord.

Remember, these times are not necessarily times for traditional prayer. They are times to "watch to see when the Lord would say". Forget your prayer-wish-list for these precious moments. The object is to hear from the Lord, whatever He wants to talk about. Let Him set the agenda for these meetings. You simply choose a venue where you can tune into the frequency of Heaven.

"I will watch to see what He will say within me"

Note that Habakkuk was not so much interested to hear, per se. He wanted to "watch to see what the Lord would say". He knew that the Lord has a variety of ways to communicate. Habakkuk did not want to eliminate or negate any of the methods the Lord could use. He was open to all of them. He activated all his spiritual senses to pick up the revelation of the Lord.

Will you "watch to see" or will you simply continue to strain your natural ears to hear. Go ahead; activate your spirit to receive all of God's revelations. Clear the projection screen of your spirit. Be alert for visions, dreams, instructions, etc.

Habakkuk also realized that the Lord would in all probability say things **within** him, in his spirit. He knew, once he quieted his spirit to receive from heaven, God would somehow speak clearly and directly to him. He was not straining for an audible expression of the voice of the Lord alone. He knew that God's inner voice carries the same authority as His external, audible voice.

Designate time to listen; to receive from the Lord so you can pass it on to others.[115] Are you desperate to hear from the Lord? Listen, your life depends on it! He is ready, willing and able to bless you with creative ideas, directional instructions and powerful abilities. He wants to illuminate your mind, activate your spirit and refresh your body. You'll be enriched, renewed and primed for life. Open the eyes of your heart. Watch to see what He will say within you!

"Write down the vision"
After all the preparation to receive instruction and vision from the Lord, what are you going to do with it once He speaks within you? The first thing the Lord told Habakkuk to do was to write

---

[115] 1Corinthians 11:23

down the vision plainly so that those who come by would be able to read it and be on their way. He was to document the vision. To preserve it in detail so it will be a blessing in days to come and to people who would read it later. If Habakkuk did not write it down as instructed, we would never have read these verses. We would not have been blessed by Habakkuk's experiences and prophecies. I would not have been able to write a portion of this book! Do you get the picture?

Show the Lord that you value what He says. Document your dreams, visions and spiritual experiences. You'll be able to read and study them without having to give up on detail you cannot remember. You'll be able to share some of those experiences with others as the Lord allows you to and be a tremendous blessing to them. If you do not like to write them down, then get a digital voice recorder. Use the great technology we have available. My point is that you want to archive your experiences with the Lord. It is truly enriching. When your prophetic promises are documented you can refer to them for encouragement and reference them for confirmation later. Remember, there is a prophetic edge to the word of God. There can be more than one fulfillment of His promises. Sometimes they are yet for an appointed time. Reference them so you can remind Him of His promises[116] to you and so you do not forget them.

Value of a Journal

I want to encourage you to maintain a spiritual journal. Put all your spiritual experiences together, either in a book or in digital format. Some people love to journal every day. Blogs (digital journals) have taken the internet by storm lately. Quiet yourself, watch to see what the Lord would say within you and then write it down. Filter your journal through the Word of God. It must harmonize with the inspired will of God as we find it in the Bible. Never elevate your spiritual journal above the authority of the Bible. If you follow these safeguards, you will find journaling to be a rewarding and wonderful blessing in your life.

---

[116] Isaiah 62:6-7

CHAPTER 5
HEAR FROM GOD INTELLIGENTLY

I love the name Samuel. It comes from two Hebrew words. "Shama"[117] means "to hear intelligently" and "El" means "God"[118]. When you put the two words together "Samuel" means "heard or to hear intelligently from God". One day while reading 1 Samuel 3 the Lord started to speak to me in no uncertain terms. He opened that passage in my spirit, and it is fair to say that it really changed my life. I have shared this teaching in many churches across America with tremendous results and now I want to share it with you.

> *NOW THE boy Samuel ministered to the Lord before Eli. The word of the Lord was rare and precious in those days; there was no*

---

[117] Strong's Exhaustive Dictionary of Bible words. OT: 8085
[118] Strong's Exhaustive Dictionary of Bible words. OT: 410

> *frequent   or   widely   spread vision.*[119]

Here we have an introduction into the forming of a formidable prophet and man of God. The boy Samuel ministered to the Lord before Eli. His mother, after a long season of barrenness promised that if the Lord would give her a son, she would give him back to God. She became pregnant and gave birth to a beautiful boy. She called him Samuel. Think about it! She chose a name that initially was prophetic in nature. Every time he would hear his name, he would also be reminded of its meaning: "You, who hear from God intelligently . . ." Now in our study text, we find him ministering to the Lord before the priest Eli. Samuel was still a young boy. In fact, the Hebrew word for boy here is "na'ar" and defines a child between infancy and adolescence.[120]

As a boy, Samuel was inexperienced but full of energy and zeal. Where he lacked knowledge and strength he made up for in potential and youthfulness. He ministered to the Lord by attending to, and serving the needs of the house of the Lord. One gets the impression that he was a diligent worker.

---

[119] 1 Samuel 3:1 AMP.
[120] Strong's Exhaustive Dictionary of Bible words. OT: 5288

> *Now Samuel **did not yet know the Lord**, and the **word of the Lord was not yet revealed to him**.*[121]

In verse one he ministers to the Lord but in verse seven we find that he did not yet know the Lord and the word of the Lord was not yet revealed to him. What an eye opener! Did you know that you can minister to the Lord and not yet know Him? How many people today may be active in church, ministering to the Lord?

Are you truly a Christian or do you just carry that name?

They may be fulfilling some or other religious action or ritual without knowing the Lord in a personal and real way; without having a revelation of the word of God in their lives. Religious activity does not ensure a relationship with God!

Here Samuel is ministering to the Lord, doing a tremendous service in the Kingdom of God, yet personally he was not living up to the meaning of his name. The one known as "he who hears from God intelligently" has not heard from the Lord just yet! He carried a name with a tremendous meaning, but was not living up to the meaning of that name.

---

[121] 1 Samuel 3:7 AMP Emphasis Added.

Are you truly a Christian or do you just carry that name?

> *. . . and in Antioch the disciples were first called **Christians**.*[122]

The Greek word "Christianos" here means "follower of Christ".[123] They who are actively following Christ live up to the meaning of the name. They adhere to His teachings, follow His example, and worship Him as King of kings and Lord of lords.

For the purposes of this book I want to use Samuel as a type of your regenerated spirit, the God-portion in you. Your spirit is the newest, youngest member of the "You-family". When you surrendered your life to Jesus, accepted Him as your Savior and invited Him into your life you were born again. Your spirit-man was regenerated. Your Samuel was born in you! Follow me on this. Your spirit has an inherent ability to hear from the Lord intelligently! God placed it there. That means that you do not need any other gift from above to hear from God, you should simply allow your Samuel to grow and develop his influence over your life. Remember he is young and mostly inexperienced, even

---

[122] Acts 11:26b AMP. Emphasis Added.
[123] Strong's Exhaustive Concordance of Bible words NT: 5547

naïve at times. But then he is full of energy. He is your connection to God and has a tremendous future before him. He loves the presence of the Lord and ministers to the Lord with diligence and great zeal. He loves to be in close proximity to the Ark of God.

> . . . *and the lamp of God had not yet gone out, and Samuel was lying down in the temple of the LORD where the ark of God was,* [124]

Your Samuel is your greatest ally to hear the voice of the Lord. Your spirit man is poised and ready. He may not have all the revealed knowledge just yet, but know this, the Lord is about to reveal His word to your spirit-man (Samuel) in a very special way!

> *At that time Eli, whose eyesight had dimmed so that he could not see, was lying down in his own place.* [125]

Eli here represents the old flesh-man; the old you. He is a type of the flesh. He is outdated, has lost his vision and sense of direction. He is

---

[124] 1 Samuel 3:3 NASB
[125] 1 Samuel 3:2 AMP.

stagnant and is lying down in his own place, while Samuel loves to rest in the presence of the Lord! Your Eli prides himself on his past. In fact, his past is always going to be greater than his future. He is all about ritual, tradition and religiosity. He goes through the mere motions of religious activity. He possesses a wealth of experience, is supposed to be the priest in the temple, but has lost his ability to hear from heaven. Interestingly enough the Hebrew word "Eli" here means "lofty". Your flesh is so filled with pride and arrogance that he never wants to acknowledge when he needs help or assistance.

We all have both a Samuel and Eli inside of us; a flesh-man and spirit-man coexisting in the same God-given temple, your body. Paul writes about this co-habitation:

> *For **I fail to practice the good deeds I desire to do, but the evil deeds that I do not desire to do are what I am [ever] doing**. So I find it to be a law (rule of action of my being) that when I want to do what is right and good, evil is ever present with me and I am subject to its insistent demands. For I endorse and delight in the Law of God in my inmost self [with my new nature]. But I*

> *discern in my bodily members [in the sensitive appetites and wills of the flesh] a different law (rule of action) at war against the law of my mind (my reason) and making me a prisoner to the law of sin that dwells in my bodily organs [in the sensitive appetites and wills of the flesh]. THEREFORE, [there is] now no condemnation (no adjudging guilty of wrong)* **for those who are in Christ Jesus, who live [and] walk not after the dictates of the flesh, but after the dictates of the Spirit.**[126]

Paul writes of a tug of war inside of him. That battle for dominance and supremacy in his life between the spirit-man and the flesh-man. The bigger one will always rule over the smaller! In 1 Samuel 3:1 we find young Samuel serving before the more established and experienced Eli. But God was settings things in place to restore vision and destiny back to the people of God. He was about to establish Samuel as one of the greatest prophets of Israel, one that would hear from God again and govern His people.

---

[126] Romans 7:19, 21-23; 8:1 AMP. Emphasis Added.

Who reigns in your life? Is it Eli or Samuel, spirit or flesh, relationship or religiosity? Paul continues:

> *THEREFORE, [there is] now no condemnation (no adjudging guilty of wrong) for those who are in Christ Jesus, **who live [and] walk not after the dictates of the flesh, but after the dictates of the Spirit.**[127]*

Clearly a life according to the dictates of the spirit is more desirable and free from condemnation. Ready your Samuel, the one who can hear from God intelligently. He is about to become the prominent dominant in your life!

Rare and Precious
The word of the Lord was rare and precious in those days and there was no widely spread vision. When you position your life so the word of the Lord becomes a rarity in your life, you will lack widely spread vision for your life and your fleshly Eli will dominate your sprit-sensitive Samuel. Today you have no excuse not to immerse your life into God's word. You can study it and allow the Lord to reveal

---

[127] Romans 8:1 AMP Emphasis Added

tremendous Kingdom depths to you. Vision starts with the word of God.

While Eli is lying down in his own place and Samuel is seeking the presence of the Lord to rest in (close to the Ark of the Covenant), the word of the Lord states an important fact:

Somewhere in the deep recesses of your heart is still some Holy Spirit oil left.

> *The lamp of God had not yet gone out in the temple of the Lord, where the ark of God was, and Samuel was lying down.* [128]

Although there was no widely spread vision, and although the priest, Eli, who were supposed to be able to hear the voice of the Lord but now had no vision, and although the word of the Lord was rare and precious in those days, the fire of God has not yet gone out in the temple! The lamp of the Lord was still burning. That means that there was still some oil in the candlestick! Hey, you might think that old Eli in you is calling the shots spiritually and small Samuel has no clue about what to do. You might even feel like the word of God has no

---

[128] 1 Samuel 3:3 AMP

impact in your life and you are without widely spread vision. You lack illumination and revelation to light your way. I've got good news for you! The lamp of God in you is not out just yet! Somewhere in the deep recesses of your heart is still some Holy Spirit oil left. God's flame in you is still burning otherwise you would not be reading this book, seeking to hear God's voice intelligently.

Friend let me tell you, a small flame has the same features and characteristics as a big fire. In fact most fires start with a small flame. Do not underestimate the now small, smoldering and dying flame. God is not done with you! He has great plans for you. Just when all seems lost in a church, God revives it! Just when things get really hopeless He steps in with miraculous results. Start to fan that flame in you.

In this toxic environment of mere human reasoning, messed up philosophies and evil endeavors God still has a voice. Just because His word has been rare and precious in the secular media does not mean that He has become mute. Remember, He stays a revealing God who loves to talk to you. That is exactly what He did with young Samuel.

When the Lord called, Samuel!
And he answered, Here I am.[129]

Regardless of the terrible spiritual environment God speaks to Samuel. Remember, this boy has never heard the voice of the Lord nor has it ever been revealed to him. Samuel was a complete novice at this. Look at the first word the Lord speaks to him: "Samuel". Protocol suggests that God would speak to the priest, after all this is in a strict Old Testament era where only the priest, king or the prophet normally heard from the Lord. If God was going to speak surely He would not leave His important message with an inexperienced boy, or would He? The Lord identifies the person He wants to communicate with by name! In the event that Eli may just hear His voice from Heaven, he would never mistake the object of the message. These words are targeted towards Samuel.

I have called you by your name;
you are Mine.[130]

The Lord knows you and calls you too by name. He redeemed you and you belong to Him. You are His! You belong! You do not have to rely on the voice of religion or tradition, your Eli, to

---

[129] 1 Samuel 3:4 AMP
[130] Isaiah 43:1b AMP

convey the messages of God to you through the dirty filtered glasses of stagnant blindness. Get them directly from the Source!

What's more here is that as the Lord called: "Samuel", He was actually prophesying into young Samuel's life. Remember Samuel means: *he who hears from God intelligently.* It has never happened in Samuel's life. He's never heard God's voice, much less in an intelligent way. The Lord has a way to speak prophetic promise into your life with simple, yet powerful words. He has a way to get your attention. Before he addresses the current state of affairs in your life He delivers a potent promise of what is to come.

Activation of a Prophetic Promise
For the first time Samuel hears the voice of the Lord! This was not a mere dream or hallucination. He responds with a: Here I am. Look at this. He did not complain at the inhuman hour of the call. He did not procrastinate with a: "I'll do it in the morning." or a typical "Five more minutes!" No, he was at the ready. His servant's heart compelled him to action.

He ran to Eli and said, Here I am,
for you called me. Eli said, I did

not call you; lie down again. So he went and lay down.[131]

What a surprisingly stupid action! God was calling yet Samuel runs to Eli. Isn't that oh so typical in our lives as well? God speaks to our spirit-man and all we want to do is to filter it through our Eli, the flesh. Samuel heard the voice of the Lord but not in an intelligent way. He took action, but in the wrong direction.

Will you stop running to the filter of religion when the voice of divine relationship beckons you? How many times have you heard from the Lord in your spirit only to be pacified and coaxed back to a deep spiritual slumber by the flesh? The Lord does not only want you to hear His voice, He wants you to hear it in an intelligent way. Samuel had the first part down, but he was having trouble with the intelligent part of his prophetic name.

The Lord called two more times with similar results. Finally, upon the third time Samuel went to Eli, the old priest came to his spiritual senses. He actually gave better advice this time. He said:

---

[131] 1 Samuel 3:5 AMP

And the Lord called Samuel the third time. And he went to Eli and said, Here I am, for you did call me. Then Eli perceived that the Lord was calling the boy. So Eli said to Samuel, Go, lie down. And if He calls you, you shall say, **Speak, Lord, for Your servant is listening.** *So Samuel went and lay down in his place.* [132]

This is a typical instruction from a religious mindset. When you've exhausted all other options and avenues, then go to God. When all else fails, trust Him. Can you hear that I am no friend of the Eli lurking in you? He led you astray many times before and wasted enough precious time in your life. He caused repeated cycles of failed communications from heaven because of his out-of-touch-with-God posture.

The Lord was doing something special and extraordinary to ensure intelligent hearing.

A New Approach

Even with the advice Eli gave Samuel, the Lord was not going to be misunderstood again. Three

---

[132] 1 Samuel 3:8-9 AMP Emphasis Added

times Samuel heard His voice unintelligently. The Lord would not allow that again!

> *And the Lord **came** and **stood** and **called** as at other times, Samuel! Samuel! Then Samuel answered, Speak, Lord, for Your servant is listening. The Lord told Samuel, Behold, I am about to do a thing in Israel at which both ears of all who hear it shall tingle.* [133]

The first three times Samuel heard the voice of the Lord it was a voice coming from the balconies of heaven. The Bible states merely that the Lord called. His voice must have traveled a tremendous distance to reach Samuel's ears. Yet, Samuel still managed to mess it up by running to Eli. Now the Lord was doing something special and extraordinary to ensure intelligent hearing. This time the Lord came and stood and called. Do you see this? Before He merely called, now He came and stood first.

This causes a tremendous excitement in my spirit. I believe the Lord is once again reverting to such extraordinary measures to get you to hear His voice intelligently! The Church has

---

[133] 1 Samuel 3:10 AMP Emphasis Added.

been running to Eli for revelation for far too long. I believe the Lord is stepping into lives again in a powerful way. He is positioning Himself between you and your Eli! This time when you run, you will run right into Him! Imagine the sound of His voice originating not from a far away heaven but from right beside you! Not only will you hear, but this time you will hear His voice intelligently!

Prepare your life for amazing encounters with the Living God. He is about to invade your private moments with divine revelations. He carries a message too important for you not to understand it. He is once again about to do a thing in your life at which both ears of all who hear it shall tingle! That is pretty powerful stuff.

What a Word!
What was this message that was so important that caused the Lord to call to Samuel 4 times? What was on God's mind? Why so persistent? What can cause your ears tingle like that?

Actually the message was two-fold. First the Lord was declaring an end to the house of Eli. The old priest's reign was over. He turned a blind eye to the sins of his sons and ended up with no real vision in his own life. He tolerated the intolerable. He held the title but lost the position of priest of Almighty God. The Lord was preparing His people for a new leader, someone who would hear His voice intelligently. God was removing Eli, announcing judgment over his household.

This is actually great news to the nation of Israel! This was no time for sentiment. Israel needed to hear from the Lord. They needed vision and someone to welcome the word of the Lord into their midst.

What is God doing in your life in this season? I believe it has to do with a removal of your Eli. He is judging the flesh, declaring an end to a fleshly reign with a worldly view in your life. Isn't that exciting? Is one of your ears tingling already? Do not mourn for Eli. He has had his change and blew it. Your flesh-man does not have what it takes to connect you to God. All he has to offer you are pride and ritual; mere religious shells with no spiritual substance. Will you allow the Lord to accomplish what He is setting out to do in you?

> *But the natural, non-spiritual man does not accept or welcome or admit into his heart the gifts and teachings and revelations of the Spirit of God, for they are folly (meaningless nonsense) to him; and he is incapable of knowing*

121

them [of progressively recognizing, understanding, and becoming better acquainted with them] because they are spiritually discerned and estimated and appreciated. But the spiritual man tries all things [he examines, investigates, inquires into, questions, and discerns all things], [134]

The apostle Paul in the book of Romans, especially chapter 8, describes the demise of the flesh and calls for life in the spirit. He recognizes the need to live your life connected to a higher standard than what your Eli (flesh) can give.

*For those who are according to **the flesh and are controlled by its unholy desires set their minds on and pursue those things which gratify the flesh***, *but those who are according to **the Spirit and are controlled by the desires of the Spirit set their minds on and seek those things which gratify the [Holy] Spirit**. Now the mind of the flesh [which is sense and*

---

[134] 1 Corinthians 2:14 – 15a AMP

reason without the Holy Spirit] is death [death that comprises all the miseries arising from sin, both here and hereafter]. But the **mind of the [Holy] Spirit is life and [soul] peace [both now and forever]**. So then those who are living the life of **the flesh** [catering to the appetites and impulses of their carnal nature] **cannot please or satisfy God**, or be acceptable to Him. But you are not living the life of the flesh, **you are living the life of the Spirit, if the [Holy] Spirit of God [really] dwells within you [directs and controls you]**. For if you live according to [the dictates of] the flesh, you will surely die. But if through the power of the [Holy] Spirit you are [habitually] putting to death (making extinct, deadening) the [evil] deeds prompted by the body, you shall [really and genuinely] live forever. **For all who are led by the Spirit of God are sons of God.** [135]

---

[135] Romans 8:5-6,8-9,13-14 AMP Emphasis Added.

The second part of this awesome message the Lord brought to Samuel was of even greater value. While judgment was declared over the house of Eli, the Lord was going to bless and establish Samuel as a spiritual leader of Israel! Although Samuel was only a boy, God was pleased with him. The Lord wanted someone who could hear His voice intelligently and to lead His people.

Make no mistake; God is fond of the Samuel in you. He gravitates towards your spirit and backs him to rule your life. He wants you to be a person of the Spirit. He would love your Samuel to be established to lead you into the destiny God has planned for you.

> *Samuel grew; the Lord was with him and let none of his words fall to the ground. And all Israel from Dan to Beersheba knew that Samuel was established to be a prophet of the Lord. And the Lord continued to appear in Shiloh, for the Lord revealed Himself to Samuel in Shiloh through the word of the Lord.* [136]

---

[136] 1 Samuel 3:19-21 AMP

The time has come for our Samuels to mature. Spiritual boys must become men! The demise of Eli made way for Samuel to grow. The Lord is with your Samuel. It is interesting to note that the Lord caused none of Samuels' words fall to the ground. In other words the Lord put power in Samuel's words. When he spoke, things happened. God caused those words to be heard. This is an amazing thought. When you hear from the Lord intelligently the Lord will cause your words to be heard in a similar way! You'll be able to express yourself in a way for people to pick up on what you say without words wasting to the ground.

When you allow the Lord to mentor your spirit-man, the Samuel in you will grow. He will gain momentum in life as well as irreplaceable experience from the hand of the Holy Spirit. You'll learn how to communicate in ways so

That is life in the spirit, getting your P's and Q's from the Lord through the Samuel in you.

your words settle in hearts of people and not in the dust of ignorance. The Samuel in you will be recognized as someone who has the tremendous ability to hear from the Lord intelligently. The other members of the "You" family will come to him for advise. Your emotions will submit to your spirit-man, along with your thoughts, mental capacities, motives, and physical body. When faced with a challenge or life-puzzle they will all congregate around your spirit-man. That, my friend, is life in the spirit, getting your P's and Q's from the Lord through the Samuel in you.

Shiloh

Another wonderful point to ponder is the place where the Lord met with Samuel. God continued to appear in Shiloh and the Lord revealed Himself to Samuel in Shiloh through the word of the Lord. The Hebrew word Shiloh here comes from "shiyloh" which means "to be at peace or tranquil"[137] Shiloh is a place where you can be at rest. A place where you are "happy, and where you prosper; a place where you are in safety." Shiloh is also a place with Messianic significance.

> *The scepter or leadership shall not depart from Judah, nor the ruler's staff from between his feet, until Shiloh [the Messiah, the Peaceful One] comes to Whom it belongs, and to Him shall be the obedience of the people.*[138]

---

[137] Strong's Exhaustive Dictionary of bible Words – OT #7886 & #7951

[138] Genesis 49:10 AMP

Shiloh is more than a place, He is a Person! Nationally this verse speaks of the coming of Jesus, the Messiah. I believe it also speaks of a deeply personal coming! The seat of authority in your life (scepter of leadership) remains in the regions of praise and celebration of Jesus (Judah means "celebrated or praise") in your life. Jesus will assume His strategic position of power in your life when you celebrate and praise Him for Who He is. Out of this praise flows obedience and how can you obey if you cannot hear from Him intelligently? How beautiful! The Lord is waiting for you in Shiloh. That is where you will receive awesome revelation through the word of God.

I find it interesting that people too often wait for the presence of a storm in their lives to seek God. They call to Him when in trouble or in need of some God-act on their behalf. God is into more than mere crisis management. He wants to commune with you in Shiloh. He wants to stir your heart and cause your ears to tingle while you are surrounded by His awesome peace and power.

Will you join me as I invite the Lord to speak to us? Let's give Him full permission to remove our Eli and establish our Samuel.

Speak Lord, your servants are listening. Make our ears tingle with powerful revelations from Your heart. Cause our Eli to crumble. We let go of our hold on mere formality and religiosity. We embrace and welcome the coming of age of Samuel. Stir our spirit to hear from you intelligently. Let us never again run to the flesh for advice. We turn to You to hear Your voice. Create a Shiloh in our lives where we can peacefully and powerfully hear your voice. Amen.

CHAPTER 6
PRODUCING POWER OF WORDS

What God says is. There is an amazing power generated from His words. His words are always successful. They never fail. He never lies. They create, construct and accomplish.

> *For My thoughts are not your thoughts, neither are your ways My ways, says the Lord. For as the heavens are higher than the earth, so are My ways higher than your ways and My thoughts than your thoughts. For as the **rain and snow** come down from the heavens, and return not there again, but water the earth and make it bring forth and sprout, that it may give seed to the sower and bread to the eater, [2 Cor 9:10.] So **shall My word be that goes forth out of My mouth**: it*

shall not return to Me void [without producing any effect, useless], but it shall accomplish that which I please and purpose, and it shall prosper in the thing for which I sent it.[139]

God is in a class of His own. No one can compare with Him in any way, shape or form. He carries the title, God, for obvious reasons. His thoughts are not your thoughts and your ways are not His ways. He is higher than you. This means that when His words are released into your life, they accomplish things in you from a new, higher vantage point. That is why they sometimes can surprise you. You may have focused on a specific area of need in your life, praying for a detailed outcome according to the only plausible solution you are aware of. Yet His perspective allows Him to send forth His words into you by way of a better route.

Rain – Immediate results

God's words are like rain. They come from the heavens, water the earth and cause a chain reaction of life to spring forth. Rain has an immediate effect. Its moisture can be measured the moment it hits the ground. Whatever it touches becomes wet. The words of God can

---

[139] Isaiah 55:8 – 11 AMP. Emphasis Added

also function like that water. It changes everything it touches. When God speaks like rain, His words generate immediate results. His words are released to get the job done without delay. You'll see quick responses and be astounded at the results. When the Lord addresses an area of your life with words like rain, you'll see and experience the refreshing it brings, along with the growth activation of the planted seed in the soil of your soul.

Snow – Delayed release

God's words can also come to you in the form of snow. Snow is frozen moisture. It has the same potential as water, but works slower. In winter snow accumulates on the mountains until the

"Snow-words" will accumulate on the mountains of your spirit until their season comes.

atmosphere or season changes. That snow is very important. It contains the water that will replenish the water tables and rivers that will provide sustenance to living creatures and plants for months to come. Snow has a delayed blessing. When the words of God come to you in the form of snow you might not see its immediate effect. Those words will accumulate on the mountains of your spirit until their season has come. This is an important thought. Get as much of the word of God into you all the time. Do not just go after the instantaneous nature of the rain-words, but also allow the snow-words to gather in your life. You may not "need" the snow-words today, but realize that you will need it in days to come. When you go through an important seasonal change at work, church or in your family, you'll need the timed-release-action those words of God can bring. Melting snow can replenish depleted areas of your life.

What do you do with the words of God in your life? Do not discard them simply because they do not seem to be working. Do not ignore them because you do not understand them. They may appear to be inactive, stagnant or even dead to you, but they are not.

> *For the Word that God speaks is alive and full of power [making it active, operative, energizing, and effective]; it is sharper than any two-edged sword, penetrating to the dividing line of the breath of life (soul) and [the immortal] spirit, and of joints and marrow [of the deepest parts of our nature], exposing and sifting and analyzing and judging the very*

> *thoughts and purposes of the heart.*[140]

Alive and Powerful
The words of God are alive. They have a pulse. The Greek word "zao"[141] is also translated "quick". The words of God revitalize and quicken. They are full of power. The Greek word here for power is "energes".[142] It means to be effectual and powerful; to be operative and to energize. It means "to be effective in causing something to happen / able to bring about"[143] God's words make things happen in your life! They add motion and motivation in your life to allow you to do exploits in the Kingdom of God. They raise you up to a whole new level of living. The Greek opposite of "energes" is "argos". "Argos" means "to be idle / ineffective / inactive".

Functions
According to our verse the word God speaks has three functions: Penetration, Separation and Illumination. It cuts through the bone to gain access to the marrow; the origin of life. There is

---

[140] Hebrews 4:12 AMP
[141] Strong's Exhaustive Dictionary of Bible Words Greek NT: 2198
[142] Strong's Exhaustive Dictionary of Bible Words Greek NT: 1756
[143] Louw and Nida Greek-English Lexicon of the NT:1756

nothing else that can penetrate like the word of God. It cuts through the chase. It sees through presumption, flows through pretense, and penetrates the very core of your being. That is the seedbed and growing place of God's words in you. The hardest heart cannot withstand its power. The meanest thought cannot divert it. The strongest ignorance cannot hide it but for a short while. God's word has cutting power. It is sharper than a two-edged sword. It is never one dimensional. One verse can bless you in many ways. The same word can touch many people according to their own personal needs at the time.

The words of God have a tremendous ability to separate and classify things in your life. It groups the important eternal things together while exposing the mundane. It does what cannot be done! It detangles soul and spirit; causing you to recognize with clear distinction the merit of each. It aids you to determine strategies and set priorities according to God's will for your life. It sifts through the motives of your soul; judging your hearts' thoughts and purposes.

It illuminates divine directions, shining a spirit-spotlight on God's destiny and plans for your life. It highlights God's will while casting a shadow over your own. It helps you to emphasize life's principles and God's Kingdom's purposed priorities so you are not caught up in the shallow mud holes of mere human endeavors.

CHAPTER 7
RHEMA AND LOGOS

The New Testament was originally written in Greek. The Greek language has two words for "word", Rhema and logos. Let's take a look at these two words as they pertain to our study of hearing from God intelligently.

Logos speaks of the written word. It defines the totality of the word, describing its completeness. Rhema is most often used for the spoken word. It denotes the living word. Rhema is a mere portion of the logos. The rhema is that portion of the logos made alive in you for a specific task or function. Logos represents the snow-words of God and rhema the rain-words. (Look at the previous chapter)

It is very important for every believer to accumulate as much Logos as possible. Read the written word of God. Assimilate the Bible into your heart. Memorize it, because your rhema-words will emerge from the logos-words in your life. The Lord will often take a portion of the logos and make it rhema to you in a given situation and season of your life.

> *But what does it say? The Word (God's message in Christ) is near you, on your lips and in your heart; that is, the Word (the message, the basis and object) of faith which we preach, [Deut 30:14.]*[144]

Here the apostle Paul uses rhema when he speaks of the word. The word is near you. You have access to the rhema of God! It is on your lips and in your heart! Tell me, what do you do with the words that God speaks? Mary, when the angel brought God's message to her about the birth of Jesus, positioned her life in accordance with the words spoken to her by the angel.

> *Then Mary said, Behold, I am the handmaiden of the Lord; let it be done to me according to **what you have said (rhema)**. And the angel left her.*[145]

---

[144] Romans 10:8 AMP
[145] Luke 1:38 AMP Emphasis Added.

She assumed a positive posture towards the words of God in her life. She knew they came from the Lord. That was established without a shadow of doubt, and because they were words from God she knew they would happen. God will have His way. Her own plans for her life were somewhat different. They did not include giving birth to the Savior of the world, getting pregnant when the Holy Spirit came over her and that before she was married to, and intimate with Joseph. But after she heard God's rhema spoken to her by the angel she embraced them. She knew she would not be able to fulfill these words. That was up to God, but she took a very positive posture towards them. She was not negative or even neutral towards them.

When the Lord speaks to you, what will your posture be? What will you do with His words? Will you say: "Impossible, not me!" or "I'll believe it when it happens" or "Lord, I embrace Your plans and will for my life. Even though I do not understand why or how, let all Your words over my life be fulfilled just as You willed." Jesus said:

> *More knowledge of God's word means a greater seedbed for the rhema words to grow*

139

> But the Comforter (Counselor,
> Helper, Intercessor, Advocate,
> Strengthener, Standby), the Holy
> Spirit, Whom the Father will send
> in My name [in My place, to
> represent Me and act on My
> behalf], He will teach you all
> things. **And He will cause you to
> recall (will remind you of, bring
> to your remembrance) everything
> I have told you.** [146]

How can the Holy Spirit remind you of what
Jesus said if you have not heard those things in
the first place? Here is another compelling
reason for us to immerse ourselves into the
Word of God, because even if you forget a
verse after reading it, the Holy Spirit can bring
it to your remembrance at the opportune time,
right when you need it. This happens to me all
the time while preaching. The Holy Spirit will
many times connect relevant verses to the
message, even verses I did not come across
while preparing that message. Verses that I read
many months before will surface as rhema for
that specific moment.

---

[146] John 14:26 AMP Emphasis Added.

So you will do well to study the logos everyday. Read and memorize as much of God's word as you can. More knowledge of God's word means a greater seedbed for the rhema words to grow in. It will give your life a foundation that is sure, strong and accurate to build upon. You'll better recognize when God speaks to you for you'll be familiar with the Spirit driving those words. The Author of the Bible is also the Author of your life!

Finally, ask the Lord to activate a rhema word in you everyday. Remember that the rhema words are like rain falling on the fields of your life. No rain, no life! Too many of God's people are living in a word-drought. There is no snow (logos) to replenish the rivers of living water and no rain to germinate the seed potential God placed in them. God wants to rain His word regularly upon your life.

Hearing God's Voice Intelligently

CHAPTER 8
PROPHECY:
IDENTIFYING DIVINE POTENTIAL IN YOU

God declares and speaks about that what He sees and wants for your life. He knows all the plans He has for you; plans to prosper you and not for evil to give you a hopeful future.[147] His destiny for you is prescribed in heaven, promised in prophetic utterance and will prevail in obedience. Even if your current stance in life is far removed from what He actually has in store for you, does not mean that you'll never see His potential in you realized!

> *Now the Angel of the Lord came and sat under the oak (terebinth) at Ophrah, which belonged to Joash the Abiezrite, and his son Gideon was beating wheat in the winepress to hide it from the*

---

[147] Jeremiah 29:17

Midianites. And the Angel of the Lord appeared to him and said to him, The Lord is with you, you mighty man of [fearless] courage.[148]

Gideon was hiding from the enemy. His current circumstances did not depict a mighty man of fearless courage. Yet, when the Lord greeted him, it was with a resounding: "The Lord is with you, you mighty man of fearless courage." Was God merely mocking him? Or was the Lord selling him a lie to make Gideon feel better amidst this bad situation? No, God does not mock and He does not lie. He targeted the potential hidden in Gideon's life. Gideon had the potential of becoming a mighty man of fearless courage. His current lack of courage fell way short of what could be in his life. God saw him as a courageous warrior who would free His people from the tyranny of the Midianites, the very enemy Gideon was hiding from.

Most often the Lord will speak to you in terms of the destiny He has for you. He will address current happenings in you with a prophetic eye on what could be in your life.

---

[148] Judges 6:11 – 12 AMP.

Conditional Guarantee

God's prophetic promises for your life will not automatically be fulfilled. They do not come with an unlimited guarantee. In fact, every one of His promises is attached to a divine condition. When you meet the condition of the promise, the promise itself is activated towards fulfillment. You have a responsibility to position yourself toward the fulfillment of your destiny. Obedience leads to blessing and more blessing demands greater obedience.

Too many people carry their prophetic promises as mere adornments in their lives, like pieces of jewelry around their necks. They love the feel of these promises and even their looks. They appreciate their potential

> *Obedience leads to blessing and more blessing demands greater obedience.*

value, but that is as far as they are prepared to go. Friend, those promises belong in your heart, surrounded with a positive attitude, obedient mindset and worshipful posture.

Since the recent restoration and resurgence of the prophetic gift in the Church, prophetic words, promises, dreams, and the like are not hard to come by. While a valuable and valid gift to the body of Christ, you must treat all prophetic words in your life with scriptural scrutiny.

> *But the spiritual man tries all things [he examines, investigates, inquires into, questions, and discerns all things,* [149]

Passing the test
Before you respond or react to a prophetic word given to you, you will do well to examine the source of that word. You have to make sure you are acting on a word that came from God. There are so many voices and God is not the only one speaking. You have a voice too, and an enemy that would love to lead you astray. Add to that the interference of people in your life, all tugging on your heart to ally with their needs. So, when it comes to receiving a prophetic word, isolate the source of that word. Make sure it is God communicating with you.

The enemy's words may sound good to the ear, but they are often times empty and presumptuous. They have an arrogant, demanding nature to them. They push you in a forceful way. They will apply pressure to your heart and stir guilt and even other unholy emotions in you. They are void of true peace

---

[149] 1 Corinthians 2:15a AMP

and compensate for this by appealing to your flesh with wild, often unrealistic promises. One Hebrew word for false prophecy used in the Old Testament means to "boil up". The enemy will cook up any brew of words, hoping you will eat up all that he says. The essence of his words will not be in harmony with the Bible, the inspired word of God. It may contain superficial biblical elements, but as a whole would run against the grain of the word of God.

God's prophetic words are characterized by being clothed in peace. They bring comfort to your spirit, build up and edify your faith while causing your spirit to soar. When the Lord uses someone else to speak prophetically into your life, it would be confirmations of what He has stirred in your heart to do already. His words would align perfectly with the essence, spirit and message of the Bible. God will never contradict Himself. Prophetic utterances cannot replace the Bible as the inspired word of God. In fact, the Lord welcomes scrutiny. He wants you to examine what He says, to ask for clarification and confirmation.

> *By the mouth of two or three witnesses the matter shall be established.*[150]

---

[150] Deuteronomy 19:15b NKJV

When evaluating a prophetic word given you by someone, first run it through your own spirit. *There are three that bear witness in heaven, the Father, the Word, and the Holy Spirit, and these three are One; and there are three that bear witness on earth: the Spirit, the water and the blood; these three agree as one.*[151] If it gels with the words of God, oozes with peace, confirms what the Lord already stirred in your heart and somehow challenges you to a life of deeper intimacy with God, then the Lord has spoken to you. Remember an obedient lifestyle causes spontaneous fulfillments. If you will occupy your heart with seeking, finding and following God in your life everyday, then those prophetic promises will become mile-markers on the road of your life. They will act as signposts to confirm that you are in full pursuit of God's destiny for your life.

Prophetic Positioning
Now that you have established the Source of your prophetic promises, you can position yourself towards their fulfillment. Know that God alone can accomplish what He has said. His destiny for you will most certainly be further than what your natural abilities will be able to extend. You need the Lord's skill, wisdom and power to unlock the doors of

---

[151] 1 John 5:7 - 8

destiny in your life. But you do have an important role to play. What you do with these prophetic promises will determine the measure of their activation in your life. Let's look at a few Biblical examples:

Mary, after receiving an amazing prophetic promise that she would give birth to the Messiah and Savior of the world, responded with:

> *Behold, I am the handmaiden of the Lord; let it be done to me according to what you have said. And the angel left her.* [152]

David repented after the prophet of God revealed the kings own weakness and sin. [153] Samuel heard the voice of the Lord and said: "Speak Lord your servant is listening."[154] Abram received prophetic instructions from the Lord.

> *NOW [in Haran] the Lord said to Abram, Go for yourself [for your own advantage] away from your country, from your relatives and*

---

[152] Luke 1:38 AMP
[153] 2 Samuel 12:1-13
[154] 1 Samuel 3:10

149

your father's house, to the land that I will show you. [155]

Abram left his country, relatives and surroundings to a place he did not know because of a prophetic promise from the Lord. He did however receive detailed instructions from the Lord. He knew it was God speaking to Him and therefore He could act.

Joseph received tremendous prophetic promises in the form of dreams the Lord gave him. According to these dreams, Joseph would one day be in a position of authority with even his own brothers bowing before him. When he shared his dreams with his family, his brothers threw him in a dry pit, and then they sold him as a slave. They thought Joseph was presumptuous and arrogant to say the least.

Position yourself to embrace God's entire will for you, even at the expense of your own.

Later Joseph ended up in a foreign jail for something he did not do! For years his natural circumstances were in direct contrast to his prophetic dreams. Yet he practiced his gifts

---

[155] Genesis 12:1 AMP

without being affected by his surroundings or situation. He could interpret dreams. Even in jail, he did. God placed favor on him wherever he was and one day he was appointed as second in charge of the mighty Egyptian empire. Eventually his brothers did bow before him![156] Tell me, what are you doing to facilitate the promises of God in your life? Are you angry at God because life has taken you in the opposite direction than the prophetic promise? Are you disappointed at the time it is taking to be fulfilled? Have you given up? Be a Joseph! Practice your life-gift with passion and dignity, believing that the Lord will come through for you!

Isaiah wrote a very important verse in this regard.

> *I have set watchmen upon your walls, O Jerusalem, who will never hold their peace day or night; you who [are His servants and by your prayers] put the Lord in remembrance [of His promises], keep not silence,*[157]

---

[156] Genesis 37 - 43
[157] Isaiah 62:6 AMP

Go ahead; put the Lord in remembrance of His promises over your life. Remind Him with your words and actions. Show Him that you believe in Him. Share your heart with Him daily. Meet His conditions and His blessings will follow in your life. Position yourself to embrace God's entire will for you, even at the expense of your own. The Lord will enable you to step into all His plans and purposes for your life as you see them unfold according to His timing and destiny for you.

CHAPTER 9
THE CREATIVE PROCESS OF GOD

The Lord has a specific order to get things done. He follows this creative process throughout the Bible. When you understand how He does things in your life, you'll understand more about who He is. It is important to recognize how this powerful process is applied to your life. It will give you tremendous perspective and anticipation of God's continuing work in you. God describes His creative process in Isaiah 48.

> *I have declared from the beginning the former things [which happened in times past to Israel]; they went forth from My mouth and I made them known; then suddenly I did them, and they came to pass [says the Lord].*[158]

---

[158] Isaiah 48:3 AMP

God is vocal about His actions in our lives. He declares them from the beginning. The Hebrew word "declared" here means "to manifest / to announce by word of mouth to one present / to expose, predict, explain, praise."[159] When God starts to do stuff in your life, He wants to make it known. He declares His intentions in a specific way. Look at the order this verse establishes. First, they went forth from God's mouth. Second, He made them known. Third, He suddenly accomplished them. And fourth, they came to pass.

"They went from My mouth"

The words that come from God's mouth carry creative power. In fact when His words are spoken, creation starts to happen. Now the Lord is not someone who randomly talks or make chit chat. Remember, what he says, is. He does not speak in a vacuum. He always releases His words in a prepared space or atmosphere.

> *IN THE beginning God (prepared, formed, fashioned, and) created the heavens and the earth. [Heb 11:3.] The earth was without form and an empty waste, and darkness was upon the face of the very great deep. The Spirit of*

---

[159] Strong's Exhaustive Dictionary of Bible Words, OT: 5046

God was moving (hovering, brooding) over the face of the waters. And God said, Let there be light; and there was light. [160]

Notice how the Holy Spirit was brooding, hovering and moving over the face of the waters. The Holy Spirit covered the earth that was without form and an empty waste. Obviously the earth needed a touch from God at the time. It needed a miracle to introduce form and life! It was the Holy Spirit who prepared it for that miracle we call creation. The Spirit of God established an incubation atmosphere where the words of God could go to work. There is a definite cooperation between the Holy Spirit and the Word of God. Together they work miracles in any given situation. The one compliments and enhances the other.

Within this prepared space, the Lord spoke. He said: "Let there be light." Immediately there was light. Light suddenly appeared from nowhere. Remember the sun was not created yet! Can you see this creative process?

Do you need a miracle? Are there empty waste places in your existence? Are some of your dreams and ambitions without form? Well,

---

[160] Genesis 1:1-3 AMP.

allow the Holy Spirit to brood over you too. Let Him establish a miracle-inviting-environment in your life. Ask the Holy Spirit to cover your waste lands with His mighty presence in preparation for the powerful words from God's mouth. This will ensure a maximized result. When God speaks over your situation a new order is established. It will be according to what he said. Your being will align with what He spoke forth. The enemy has to submit to God's sayings over you. Circumstances have to bow at the sound of His released words.

"And I made them known"
The second step in the creative process of God is equally powerful. Once the Lord has spoken over your life, He will work to make His words known to you. Remember how Samuel heard the voice from heaven, but did not understand Who was calling him? The meaning of Samuel's name is "to hear from the Lord intelligently", but Samuel for a while heard God's voice unintelligently. He kept running to Eli, who in turn sent him right back to bed.

The Hebrew word "to make them known" here in Isaiah 48:3 is the word "shama". It literally means "to hear intelligently". How wonderful! Not only does God speak over our lives in the presence of the Holy Spirit, He also brings explanation to His words so you can hear them in an intelligent way! The intelligence referred to here is not mere humanistic understanding. *The natural man does not discern spiritual things.* [161] The Lord will reveal to you His words over your life with a *spirit of wisdom and revelation [of insight into mysteries and secrets] in the [deep and intimate] knowledge of Him.* [162] The Lord causes us to hear His words intelligently. This "making known" process happens in you as revelation or illumination, it can be in the form of dreams and visions, or even godly advice from a mentor. It may happen as a prophetic utterance or divine thought that just popped up in your mind. Regardless of the methods the Lord might use, the end result always gives you a divine perspective on what the Lord is about to accomplish in your life.

Remember, you do not have to understand it all. In fact, there will probably be a lot of what **God is a God of suddenlies.** God does in you that will always baffle your mind. The Lord will however make known to you what He will do according to what He has spoken over your life.

---

[161] 1 Corinthians 2:14
[162] Ephesians 1:17 AMP.

157

"Suddenly I did them"

God is a God of suddenlies. He specializes in them. No amount of preparation can actually prepare you for a suddenly. The disciples spent 10 days in the upper room, praying, seeking God, and waiting for the promise from heaven. Then, one morning, when the day of Pentecost had fully come they were all assembled together when **suddenly** there was the sound of a mighty wind, fire fell on all of them, they were all filled with the Holy Spirit and each spoke in a heavenly language as the Holy Spirit enabled them.[163] They were prepared for some of it. They anticipated a tremendous happening, but nothing could prepare them for a new language. Nowhere in scripture did God say as much. Joel prophesied about this day, but his prophecy failed to mention tongues.[164] It just happened. It was part of the suddenly. There are many more suddenly moments recorded in scripture. Divine moments where promises are fulfilled and miracles happen.

The suddenly-moment also implies the mystery of God's timing. We try to synchronize our lives with the calendar of heaven, but are not always successful. We fail to anticipate and predict the specific time and manifestation of

---

[163] Acts 2:1-4
[164] Joel 2:28-32

158

the promises of God. They often times are sprung on us suddenly when we least expect them to happen. Instead of growing frustrated or even disillusioned with this, position your life to embrace the suddenlies of God. Set yourself up to positively expect surprises from heaven anywhere and at any time. Besides, a suddenly is not a complete surprise. It is a fulfillment of what you already expect God to do in you because of the words He spoke over you!

"They came to pass"
God always does what he says. He is no liar and will not deceive you. No matter how big or how small, every promise He has given you has the potential to come to pass. It is useful to remember that often times we ourselves are in the way of seeing their fulfillment. Faith activates the blessings of God and sets us up for the fulfillment of His promises. We need to keep our heart-motives pure before the Lord, while keeping our faith activated to obey His will for our lives. We should pursue relationship with God with worship and wonder; devotion and dedication; respect and reverence.

The purpose of prophetic preparation

Therefore I have declared things
to come to you *from of old;*

159

> ***before they came to pass I
> announced them to you**, so that
> you could not say, My idol has
> done them, and my graven image
> and my molten image have
> commanded them.*[165]

God's words are the driving force of things
coming to you. They set motion to His
promises, steering them towards you. They
determine the right intersection to meet you in
your circumstances. You should be able to see
them coming! Spiritually you'll be aware that
"something's up" before they happen.

There is a distinct purpose to this divine
preparation. When prophecies are fulfilled and
promises manifested in your life, God has the
honor of being able to say: "I told you so."
What has happened did not come to you
because of some dumb luck or by the hand of
another. God declared what He was going to do
and He did it. All glory and recognition must go
to Him!

It was December 9, 1994. I was on my knees in
the prayer-tower, a room in our church in South
Africa, specifically dedicated to prayer.
Suddenly I became aware of the awesome

---

[165] Isaiah 48:5 AMP Emphases Added.

manifest presence of God. An ordinary moment became an extraordinary encounter. "Son, work on your English because I am sending you to America." His words rang in my spirit with deft clarity. I documented what the Holy Spirit was saying with particular fervor to accuracy. I did not want to miss anything and I knew that in time to come I would want to re-visit the encounter in the finest details. That day the Lord addressed several things concerning our lives, ministry and destiny that forever changed us. I remember asking the Lord how He would accomplish all these marvelous, and greater-than-our-natural-abilities prophetic promises. "Next year this time you will be amazed at what I will do, and every year henceforth!" I looked at my watch and recorded the time. It was 3:00 PM.

During the next 12 months the Lord continued to work in our lives while burning a zeal for evangelism in our spirits. So much happened that year! We were revived and thrust onto a whole new level of Holy Spirit ministry. We saw a mighty wave of God rushing through our church, setting hearts ablaze for the Gospel of Jesus Christ. We saw miracles, signs and wonders, healings, salvations and amazing spiritual and numerical growth. We saw how the Lord opened up a door to America for us without our help at all! Of course many people were astounded when we declared publicly our intentions to follow the prompting of the Holy Spirit to base our ministry in America. Some even said they thought we had gone mad to even consider such a thing.

We faithfully forged ahead, packed our belongings and sent our furniture into storage. On the day that the last truck, filled with our earthly goods, left our driveway I remember looking at my watch. It was 3:00 PM. "Honey, what is today's date?" I asked in amazement. "Why it is December 9." She exclaimed. Suddenly the words of the Holy Spirit rang in my heart again. "Next year this time you will be amazed at what I will do!" We could not but give God all the glory. Only He could orchestrate such a thing! The following year we received an letter from our denomination in South Africa, in which they officially recognized and blessed God's Glory Ministries International. That letter was dated December 9, 1996! In 1997, on that very same December day we received a package in the mail containing the proofs of Sharon's first CD, Songs from the Heart. I can go on and on! The Lord has proven His words to us in so many ways. Just thinking about all that He has done each year

There are blessings, answers, power and wisdom on their way to you

leaves us speechless and amazed! And may I add again, all glory, honor and recognition must go to Him, the King of kings and Lord of lords!

They Are On Their Way!
Friend, there are blessings, answers, power and wisdom on their way to you! They were packaged in the throne room of heaven, shipped at the declaration and direction of the Lord, and now are en-route to fulfill God's will for your life.

> *You have heard [these things foretold], now you see this fulfillment. **And will you not bear witness to it?** I show you specified new things from this time forth, even hidden things [kept in reserve] which you have not known. **They are created now [called into being by the prophetic word], and not long ago;** and before today you have never heard of them, lest you should say, Behold, I knew them!*[166]

Will you position your life to receive these tremendous fulfillments? They are

---

[166] Isaiah 48:6-7 AMP Emphasis Added.

magnificently planned and powerfully packaged for your life. Will you bear witness to them? The Hebrew word for witness here is "nagad" and means "to manifest / to announce by word of mouth / to declare"[167] The Lord wants you to align your spirit with His declared promises over your life. Speak of the things that are not as if they are![168] The declarations of your mouth have a tremendous influential effect. Joseph talked about the prophetic dreams God gave him. He was not bragging or boasting before his family about them. He was merely agreeing with, and aligning his life alongside God's promises for his life. Faith rises in you when you hear the word of God![169]

I have always believed it a good practice to read God's word aloud, even when you are alone. The sound of those promises adds spirit potency to them and triggers the activation towards their fulfillment. The Lord is quite willing to share with you from His infinite reservoir of divine wisdom, knowledge, power and potential. He is a revealing God and most often will not hesitate to orchestrate things in your life according to His purposes and plans for you through the potency of prophetic utterance.

---

[167] Strong's Exhaustive Dictionary of Bible Words OT: 5046
[168] Romans 4:17b
[169] Romans 10:17 The Greek word for "word" here is "rhema" – a spoken word

They shall speak of the glory of Your kingdom and talk of Your power, To make known to the sons of men God's mighty deeds and the glorious majesty of His kingdom.[170]

The time has come for the people of God to make divine declarations; to speak of His mighty glory and power. The Lord has already made His plans known. He has spoken over your life, declared His will and mission for you. Go ahead and agree wholeheartedly and verbally with Him! Dare to believe that He will accomplish the impossible through you! Activate your faith and demonstrate it by the words flowing from your mouth.

---

[170] Psalm 145:11-12 AMP

CHAPTER 10
JESUS IS THE WORD OF GOD

We have seen already that the word of God is more than mere paragraphs. It comes to us in various forms and in a variety of ways. But I want us to take it another step further. Consider the fact that God's word has a personality; a specific and very special character. His word is a person and that person is Jesus Christ!

> *IN THE beginning [before all time] was the Word (Christ), and the Word was with God, **and the Word was God Himself**. [Isa 9:6.] He was present originally with God. All things were made and came into existence through Him; and without Him was not even one thing made that has come into being. **In Him was Life, and the Life was the Light of men. And the Light shines on***

> **in the darkness,** *for the darkness has never overpowered it [put it out or absorbed it or appropriated it, and is unreceptive to it].* [171]

When you hear God's Word you actually listen to Jesus. When you welcome His Word you are welcoming the person of Jesus Christ into your life. He is Life and Light. Not only did He shine on a cross outside of Jerusalem 2000 years ago while paying the price for your sins and mine, He is shining today in the hearts of those who believe in Him and willingly welcomed Him into their lives.

What do you do with Jesus?

Ever since He has walked the dusty roads of the Promised Land He has been a highly controversial figure. Some people tried from the beginning to put Him out of the way. [172] Some have tried to ignore Him, even denied His existence while others found solace and peace with Jesus, worshipping Him as Savior of the world. Where

> *We are to position our lives so God's word can prick up our ears.*

---

[171] John 1:1-5 AMP Emphases added.
[172] Acts 10:39

is His proper place in society? Better yet, where is His proper place in our lives? What should we do with Jesus, the very Word of God?

My son, attend to my words; consent and submit to my sayings. Let them not depart from your sight; keep them in the center of your heart, for they are life to those who find them, healing and health to all their flesh. [173]

The Bible is very clear about the precise treatment of God's words in our lives. First we must attend to them. The Hebrew word here is "qashab" and means "to prick up the ears / to hearken / to mark well / to regard"[174] We are to position our lives so God's word can prick up our ears. We must strain to hearken them; marking their message well in our hearts. We cannot simply hear but not listen. We cannot wait for their arrival and when they reach our lives after a long journey from the throne room of heaven not attend to them. Secondly we are to submit to God's sayings. We have to establish rank and president over our lives. Award the stars of the general to the word of God in your life. Then His orders will carry

---

[173] Proverbs 4:20-22 AMP.
[174] Strong's Exhaustive Dictionary of Bible Words OT: 7181

authority and credence above all else. Our verse implores us to not let His words depart from our sight. Again the Bible connects God's words to our sight and not only to our hearing. Keep your eyes on Jesus who is the Leader, Source and Finisher of our faith.[175] Set your mind on what is above, seeking and aiming at the rich eternal treasure that are above where Christ is.[176]

The Center of Your Heart
Scripturally your heart is of great value. It is the reservoir of the entire life-power.[177] In fact the Hebrew word for heart is "leb" and means "the center of everything"[178] The proper place for the word of God is thus the center of the center of your being! God cannot be more specific here! Jesus must occupy this precise and prominent place. He is the Cornerstone that holds things together in your life. He is the Pillar that carries all the weight and upholds your existence. He must be middle and center. He can never be a side issue or fleeting thought. Fact is there is a God-shaped gap in the center of your being so large that only Jesus can fill it. Nothing else can satisfy or fill this place. Without Jesus in the center of your heart your life will be lob-sided, unbalanced, and out of

---

[175] Hebrews 12:2 AMP.
[176] Colossians 3:1-2 AMP.
[177] New Unger's Bible Dictionary: Heart
[178] Strong's Exhaustive Dictionary of Bible Words OT: 3820

whack. God's words are life to those who find them and healing to their flesh! Yes, there is healing virtue in God's words, after all Jesus (The Word) is the Healer. Is the center of your heart occupied? Have you reserved it exclusively for Jesus Christ?

Springs of Life

> *Keep and guard your heart with all vigilance and above all that you guard, for out of it flows the springs of life.*[179]

Your life is defined with what comes from your heart. It is like a river producing life-water to the rest of your being. Your mind, emotions and faculties all drink from what flows from your heart, hence the importance to guard and keep your heart. To guard your heart means "to protect, maintain and obey it."[180] It also means "to watch over it and protect it from dangers and to keep secret".[181] It is obvious that this is a valuable place in your being worth to watch over and protect.

---

[179] Proverbs 4:23 AMP.
[180] Strong's Exhaustive Dictionary of Bible Words OT: 5341
[181] Brown-Driver-Brigg's Hebrew Lexicon OT: 5341

If the source (your heart) is contaminated, your whole being will suffer. It makes me think of the Israelites' encounter with bitter water:

> *When they came to Marah, they* **could not drink its waters for they were bitter;** *therefore it was named Marah [bitterness]. The people murmured against Moses, saying: What shall we drink? And he cried to the Lord, and the* **Lord showed him a tree which he cast into the waters, and the waters were made sweet.** [182]

The people of God were in a dessert and in desperate need of water. Without it they would not last long. After three long days they found water. It looked good to the eye, had the consistency of refreshing moisture, was in fact water, but the water was bitter. They could not and would not drink of it! It was so terrible they called the place Marah, which means bitterness.

Have you ever drank from the water flowing from your heart and were repulsed at the taste of it? Have you ever been disappointed at the things flowing from deep within your being to the surface of your life? Out of the abundance

---

[182] Exodus 15:23-25a AMP. Emphases Added.

of your heart your mouth will speak. [183] Whatever is in the center of your being (your heart) will manifest in your speech and behavior. Hurting people hurt people! Instead of springs of life there are gushers of bitterness, unforgiveness, sin and the like. No person in their right mind will want to camp on the beach around this Marah!

The Cure is in the Tree
Something had to be done for the Israelites. The need for fresh water was not negotiable. It could not be delayed. God, as always, had an amazing answer. He showed Moses a tree. Moses threw that tree into the bitter water and the same water became marvelously sweet! The cure for the bitterness flowing from your heart is still the same today as it was back then. The tree that brought sweetness in the place of bitterness is symbolic of Jesus! Follow me on this:

> For [the Servant of God] **grew up before Him like a tender plant, and like a root out of dry ground;** He has no form or comeliness [royal, kingly pomp], that we should look at Him, and no beauty that we should desire Him. [184]

---

[183] Matthew 12:34
[184] Isaiah 53:2 AMP. Emphasis added.

Jesus here is typified by a tender plant, a tree that grew out of dry ground.

> *And say to him, Thus says the Lord of hosts: [You, Joshua] behold (look at, keep in sight, watch)* **the Man [the Messiah] whose name is the Branch, for He shall grow up in His place** *and He shall build the [true] temple of the Lord.*[185]

Again Jesus, the Messiah, is referred to by the prophet Zechariah as the Branch that would grow up in His place. There are other references confirming this connection as well. Isaiah prophesied about the coming Messiah that there shall come forth a Shoot out of the stock of Jesse (David's father), and a Branch out of his roots shall grow and bear fruit. The Spirit of the Lord would rest upon Him.[186] Jesus is that Messiah, the Savior Who saves! Jeremiah also called the Messiah a "righteous Branch (Sprout) that will

> *It is remarkably clear that Jesus is the Branch, the tree able to transform the water flowing from your heart*

---

[185] Zechariah 6:12 AMP.
[186] Isaiah 11:1

174

reign as King and do wisely and will execute justice and righteousness in the land."[187] In Matthew 2:23 we read that Jesus deliberately dwelt in the town of Nazareth so that what was spoken through the prophets might be fulfilled: "He shall be called a Nazarene." The word Nazarene comes from Nazareth and the Hebrew word is "Netzer" and means "despised one or a branch"[188] It is remarkably clear that Jesus is the Branch, the tree able to transform the water flowing from your heart. Plant the Tree of life in your heart; position Jesus in the center of your being. He is the One who can transform every bitter area of your life into a sweet refreshing and life sustaining substance.

The river of life flows from the throne of God.[189] When we place the throne of God in the center of our heart, a river of life will spring up and start to flow through our lives.

He who believes in Me [who cleaves to and trusts in and relies on Me] as the Scripture has said, From his innermost being shall flow [continuously] springs and rivers of living water.[190]

---

[187] Jeremiah 23:5 and 33:15 AMP.
[188] New Unger's Bible Dictionary: Nazarene
[189] Revelation 22:1
[190] John 7:38 AMP.

Are you thirsty for living water? Activate your faith in Christ. Appropriate it in your life. Imagine a life free from bitterness and filled with the sweetness of Heaven! I pray that the springs of life will flow from your innermost being everyday for the rest of your life. Remember, it all starts with what you do with the words of God in your life; with what you do with Jesus! Do not be satisfied that He is a central figure in human history, He is more than that. Do not settle for a historical belief in the good things He did many years ago. He is more than that. Invite and incorporate His awesome stature and complete presence into your heart. Accept Him as your Savior, welcome His as your God and submit to Him as your Master today.

CHAPTER 11
THE VOICE OF GOD AND AN OPEN HEAVEN

Throughout the ages of time humanity has been on a quest to gain access to heaven. People have aspired to make it to this wonderful place that has no equal. Heaven is a place where the absence of all deficiencies is amplified by the presence of wholeness and completeness; a place where one's potential is realized in totality. After all it is the abode of God. Did you know that heaven has boundaries and a door? Access is gained exclusively through this door. There is no other way in. Jesus said:

> *Jesus said to him, I am the Way and the Truth and the Life; no one comes to the Father except by (through) Me.* [191]

---

[191] John 14:6 AMP

He was having a conversation with His disciples about His departure from this natural existence. He was about to pay the price for your sins and mine on the cross of Calvary. He would give up His life here to return to His original home, heaven. He wanted to comfort His followers before the most dramatic events in human history would unfold before their very eyes. What they perceived as shockingly bad news, Jesus emphasized as good news. He said: "Let not your hearts be troubled. You believe in God, believe also in Me . . . I am going to prepare a place for you in heaven!"[192] He continued to encourage them by saying: "And when I go and make ready a place for you, I will come back and will take you to Myself, that where I am you may be also."[193] Someone once said: "If God made the earth and its splendor in 7 days just imagine what heaven will be like after 2,000 years of preparation!" A wonderful thought indeed, but we do not have to wait until we cross that proverbial Jordan to gain access to this wonderful place. Many of this present life's blessings flow through the windows of heaven over your life.

> *Bring all the tithes (the whole tenth of your income) into the*

---

[192] John 14:1, 2 AMP
[193] John 14:3 AMP

*storehouse, that there may be food in My house, and prove Me now by it, says the Lord of hosts, if I will not **open the windows of heaven for you and pour you out a blessing, that there shall not be room enough to receive it.**[194]*

According to Genesis 7:11 rain falls through the windows of heaven. Windows can be opened or shut. Can it be that in the absence of blessings flowing in your life and even in the absence of rain, that the Lord closed the windows of heaven over your life or a region for some or other reason? Can it be that our response toward God's word can compel Him to maintain an open heaven over our lives?

*And if in spite of all this you still will not listen and be obedient to Me, then I will chastise and discipline you seven times more for your sins. And I will break and humble your pride in your power, and **I will make your heavens as iron [yielding no answer, no blessing, no rain] and your earth [as sterile] as brass.**[195]*

---

[194] Malachi 3:10 AMP Emphasis Added.
[195] Leviticus 26:18-19 AMP Emphasis Added.

The answer to my pondering questions above is a resounding: Yes! Our behavior do indeed influence and even determine whether we have an open or closed heaven over our lives. In Deuteronomy 28 the Lord declares with remarkable clarity the rewards for obedience and disobedience.

> *Your ability to hear the voice of the Lord is crucial to have an open heaven over your life*

Disobedience will result in, among other terrible things that "the heavens over your head shall be brass and the earth under you shall be iron."[196] Obedience on the other hand will cause, among other tremendous blessings an open heaven over your life. In fact, your ability to hear the voice of the Lord is crucial to have an open heaven over your life!

> *IF YOU will listen diligently to the voice of the Lord your God, being watchful to do all His commandments which I command you this day, the Lord your God will set you high above all the nations of the earth. And all these blessings shall come upon you and overtake you if you heed the voice of the Lord your God.*

---

[196] Deuteronomy 28:23 AMP

> *The Lord shall open to you His good treasury, the heavens, to give the rain of your land in its season and to bless all the work of your hands; and you shall lend to many nations, but you shall not borrow. And the Lord shall make you the head, and not the tail; and you shall be above only, and you shall not be beneath, if you heed the commandments of the Lord your God which I command you this day and are watchful to do them.* [197]

The Lord wants you to be happy and to walk in His awesome blessings, but He also wants you to obey His word and listen to His voice. The amazing thing is that He makes it easy to hear His voice. Obedience is as easy as self surrender. It is only complicated when pride is steering your heart. To obey is a follower's second nature.

In life, believers should take charge and lead by being an example to others, but in worship and the presence of God we are to follow the One who knows how to successfully navigate creation. We gain our leadership skills from the

---

[197] Deuteronomy 28: 1-2, 12-13 AMP Emphasis Added.

God we follow. We imitate Him in words, actions and deeds.

God is inclined to maintain an open heaven over your life while your natural tendency is to keep your heart's door closed, mainly for security reasons. You force God's hand to close heaven's door through your actions of disobedience and stubbornness while He often times have to knock on your heart's door to remind you to give Him access into your life.

> *Behold, I stand at the door and knock; if anyone hears and listens to and heeds My voice and opens the door, I will come in to him and will eat with him, and he [will eat] with Me.*[198]

The fact is that doors are opened, both in heaven and in your heart, through your ability to hear the voice of the Lord. If you hear and listen to and heed God's voice as he knocks on your heart's door you will open that door and He will come in to share wonderful times of fellowship and companionship with you. Did you notice in this verse there is food involved? He wants to eat with you. Jesus said: "My food is to do the will of Him who sent Me, and to

---

[198] Revelation 3:20 AMP

finish His work."[199] The disciples wanted to give Jesus food to eat; instead He made the impacting remark mentioned above. If Jesus is sustained and satisfied by doing the will of His Father, will you be sustained and satisfied by doing His will as well?

> *After these things I looked, and behold, a door standing open in heaven. And the first voice which I heard was like a trumpet speaking with me, saying, "Come up here, and I will show you things which must take place after this."*[200]

Listening to God's voice secures an open door in Heaven over your life, and having heaven's door opened in your life ensures that you will hear His voice. Your place is being prepared over yonder and today you have an invitation to stopover, to inspect, and to experience the blessed bliss of absolute eternity within the frailty of your current existence.

Will you hear His voice? Will you listen to His instruction? Can you see the tremendous open door of destiny and what it will give you access

---

[199] John 4:34 AMP
[200] Revelation 4:1 AMP

to? Step towards that door. In fact, step through it. Follow and obey the voice of the Lord as He beckons you to greater places, deeper realities and more glorious experiences. Incline your ears to catch and hold on to even His whispers. Ready your heart to respond to His slightest suggestions. Anchor your feet to walk in the direction of His presence.

CHAPTER 12
TODAY IF YOU WILL HEAR HIS VOICE

Hearing God's voice in your life is not optional. If you want to excel in divine destiny, and be completely satisfied and fulfilled in your life while touching many others and making a difference in their lives, you simply must hear from heaven. Do not put it on your to do list for tomorrow. Do not put it off. Why would you want to put it off?

> *Today, if you would hear His voice and when you hear it, do not harden your hearts as in the rebellion [in the desert, when the people provoked and irritated and embittered God against them]. [Ps 95:7,8.] For who were they who heard and yet were rebellious and provoked [Him]? Was it not all those who came out of Egypt led by Moses? And with whom was He irritated and*

provoked and grieved for forty years? Was it not with those who sinned, whose dismembered bodies were strewn and left in the desert? **And to whom did He swear that they should not enter His rest, but to those who disobeyed [who had not listened to His word and who refused to be compliant or be persuaded]?**[201]

Today is the best time to hear God's voice intelligently. Yesterday has vanished from the radar screen of time and cannot be re-visited ever again. It is forever behind you. Tomorrow dangles before you like the proverbial carrot on a stick. No matter how much you reach for it, it will always stay just beyond today's setting sun. You've had a yesterday, you may have another tomorrow, but you are living in today.

The Bible is clear. Today, if you will hear His voice. . . These powerful words tell us that God is speaking today. He is communicating with you this very moment. Will you train your attention to receive His instruction? Amazingly Hebrews 3:15 refers to the Israelites whom the Lord delivered from the tyranny of Egypt and

---

[201] Hebrews 3:15-18 AMP Emphasis Added

was leading to a Promised Land they could call their own. He wrought many miracles, performed feats in plain sight of the people. Actions reserved exclusively for Almighty God. They saw His mighty hand as He marvelously made a way for them through a desolate wilderness en-route to the fulfillment of His wonderful promise to them. They heard His voice but did not listen to His instruction. Time after time they provoked His wrath because of their stubborn disobedience. The result was desert-living. That generation never stepped into the rest of God. They were plagued with weaknesses, constantly fighting enemies, always in search of sustenance while living in an atmosphere of drought. They faced battles internally while the fulfillment of that great promise remained somewhere in their tomorrow.

Does this sound like a fun and fulfilled life? Is this the kind of existence to be desired? Friend, there is a much better way to live! Listen to God's voice today. Do not harden your heart. Stop ignoring His instruction. The Lord does not want to clip your freedom wings. In fact He wants to broaden your horizons! He does not want to limit your

> **God does not want to limit your life. He wants to expand it**

life. He wants to expand it! His voice will never subtract from you, it will add to you.

> *Come now, and let us reason together, says the Lord. Though your sins are like scarlet, they shall be as white as snow; though they are red like crimson, they shall be like wool. If you are willing and obedient, you shall eat the good of the land; But if you refuse and rebel, you will be devoured by the sword. For the mouth of the Lord has spoken it.* [202]

The grammar of this verse places its message right in front of you this very moment. Have you ever had something fall into your lap? You just have. Come now, let us reason together, says the Lord. Postponements are out of the question. There is an urgency attached to this. Sin poses a grave danger in your life. If you become aware of a bomb hidden in your vehicle about to explode, will you still drive it? No, you will get away from that danger immediately. You will even leave personal articles behind only to rush to safety. Things can be replaced, but your life is priceless. Why would you

---

[202] Isaiah 1:18-20 AMP

tolerate something in your life that carries the price of death? Why ignore the time-bomb of destruction the Bible calls sin?

What is sin?

Sin is all that is present in your life that should not be there. Take a tour through your life with your conscience as a guide. You will quickly become aware of things you've said and done that were not wholesome at all. You'll see the craters these bombs have created in areas of your life. The destruction and devastation will be apparent. *We all have sinned and fall short of the Glory of God.*[203] The Greek word for sin in this verse is *hamatano* and means *to miss the mark (and so not share in the prize)*[204]. You were supposed to hit the target of God's destiny for your life, but you missed. You were supposed to be a winner, but you were defeated and lost the reward of a great prize. You have sinned! You allowed the enemy of your soul to attach deadly substances to your life that will cause you to fall way short of what you were created for, the glory of God. How long will you live like this?

Deal with it immediately

---

[203] Romans 3:23

[204] Strong's Exhaustive Dictionary of Bible Words, NT:264

Come now, let us reason together, says the Lord. Though your sins are like scarlet, they shall be as white as snow; though they are red like crimson, they shall be like wool. God is the only expert qualified and able to remove sin from your life. The lines of life and eternity run parallel with each other. You can cross over at any time and when you do, all sin present that was unattended to in life will be dealt with in no uncertain terms.

> *For the wages which sin pays is death, but the [bountiful] free gift of God is eternal life through (in union with) Jesus Christ our Lord.*[205]

This verse applies to saint and sinner alike. Sometimes it seems to me that Christians tolerate sin in their lives, thinking that somehow they will receive a get-out-of-jail pass at heaven's door. They tend to forget that sin is serious business. Sin must be confessed and addressed.[206] Only the blood of Jesus cleanses of all sin.[207] Sin enslaves its victims[208] and ties their lives to eternal death. To ignore it is dangerous and irresponsible; to tolerate it in

---

[205] Romans 6:23 AMP
[206] 1 John 1:8-10
[207] 1 John 1:7
[208] John 8:34

your life is reprehensible and foolish. You will do good to become "allergic" to it. Keep it out as best you can and confess it the moment it gains forcible entry to your heart. Do not allow it to conceal itself or find a quiet spot in your life to grow. Submit your life to God and resist the devil and he will flee from you![209] So, without any further delay, allow the Holy Spirit to search through your life. When He detects any sin He will convince you of it right away. Then simply confess them to God. Bring them out in the open and ask for God's forgiveness, based on the marvelous sacrificial work of Jesus on the cross. He is your Redeemer; someone who, when sin was found in you, stepped in to receive the punishment of death handed to you. He died for your sins so you do not have to. His gift to you is eternal life in union with Jesus Christ.

Know His voice

> *When he has brought his own sheep outside, he walks on before them, and the sheep follow him because they know his voice. They will never [on any account] follow a stranger, but will run away from him because they do*

---

[209] James 4:7

> *not know the voice of strangers or recognize their call.*[210]

Sheep are never driven like cattle. They are led. Jesus calls His followers sheep. He uses this illustration to reveal something about Him as well as His followers. Although He is Almighty God and omnipotent He is not dictatorial in His dealings with humanity. He is the Good Shepherd.[211] He leads

He always leads the sheep with the sound of His voice

people safely to their divine destiny. He accompanies them and He protects them on the way. When one strays from the desired path and looses their way, He corrects lovingly and decisively. He has a Shepherd's staff and rod, but uses His voice to lead. The staff and rod are to comfort His followers.[212] In Biblical times a good shepherd's staff represented authority and was a sign of rank. Sometimes it was inscribed with the owner's name. It was also used as an aid in climbing hills, beating bushes and low brush in which the flock sometimes strayed, and where snakes and reptiles abounded.[213]

---

[210] John 10:4-5 AMP
[211] John 10:11, 14
[212] Psalm 23:4
[213] New Unger's Bible Dictionary, "Staff" Hebrew: matteh, maqqel, shebet. Greek: hrabdos.

Most of us would be tempted to, in moments of frustration to use this rod and staff to punish the sheep with, but the Lord never does. He'll beat the enemy who attacks the sheep like a serpent in ambush under a bush. He'll use the crook on the end of His staff to draw a lamb away from a danger zone but He always leads the sheep with the sound of His voice!

Do you know the sound of His voice? Will you follow that sound? Instead of walking after a fad follow God's voice in your life. You will find He will lead you into the immediate direction you need to go and with an eye on your future destiny.

PRAYER OF SALVATION

Heavenly Father, I come to You admitting that I am a sinner and fall short of the glory only You can give. I ask You to cleanse me of all sin. Please wipe away my past failures.

Let me see and experience what Kingdom living is all about. I call on the Name of Jesus Christ, my Lord and Savior to save my life this very moment. I choose to follow You and live my life to the fullest to bring pleasure to You.

I have heard the sound of Your voice and submit my life to You. Teach me Your ways and lead me according to Your will for my life. Jesus, You believed in me when nobody else did. Now I believe in You!

I declare that from this moment I am Your child. I am saved from sin. I have been born again, in Jesus' mighty Name,   Amen.

A Final Word

Thank you for reading this book. I trust that it blessed you as much as it blessed me writing it. I pray that you will hear God's voice intelligently on a continual basis. May the Lord stir you to the greatness of His word in you. May He use you according to the absolute potential of His declared word. May your life stir many to submit to the Lord and hear His voice as well!

If you have prayed the prayer of salvation, or if this book has changed your life, I would love to hear from you. Please write me at:

God's Glory Ministries International, Inc.
P. O. Box 1430
Dacula
GA 30019
You can also visit us on the web at
GodsGlory.org
Here you can send me an e-mail or browse our site for tremendous ministry materials, and even listen to podcasts.

ABOUL LHE AULHOR

Dr. Rudi Swanepoel was born in South Africa. He came to the USA in 1996 under a mandate of the Holy Spirit. Rudi, along with his wife Sharon, founded God's Glory Ministries International in 1997. Thousands are touched by the love of Jesus through services, crusades, humanitarian endeavors, education and media distribution. A seasoned evangelist, anointed preacher and friend to the next generation, Rudi's passion for God ignites people to fervency for the cause of the Kingdom. Rudi has a unique and powerful prophetic message to the corporate church. His insights into the Word of God allow him to reach into the hearts of his listeners, connecting them to the heart of God. His message is current, relevant and understandable to all. He delivers his message, spoken or written, with tremendous clarity and flowing with the anointing God placed on his life. Rudi attained a Doctorate in Ministry from CLU in 2003. His passion to see a lost humanity transformed by the power of God drives him to pursue the greater things of the Kingdom. He resides in the United State of America in Atlanta, Georgia.

Other books written by the Author

Divine Reality

When mere truth becomes reality. It tells the story of Gideon, how he was changed from a fearful man, cowardly hiding from the enemy to a powerful man of God. With many real life testimonies and practical applications from Rudi & Sharon's lives this book comes alive to stir the reader to a changed life in the reality of Who God is. Available today at www.GodsGlory.org or www.amazon.com

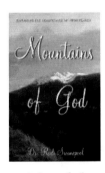

Mountains of God

The greatest events that shaped the course of history and humanity occurred on mountains. This book recreates these momentous mountain moments and leads the reader to the apex of spiritual experience. In his unique riveting writing style, Rudi explores the importance of climbing these same mountains in a quest to partake of the glories God made available to those explorers of the greater things of the Kingdom of Heaven. Available today at www.GodsGlory.org